The
ICEBERG
You Don't See

The
ICEBERG
You Don't See

The Marketing System for Financial Advisors

RODGER FRIEDMAN
& PARTHIV SHAH

ACKNOWLEDGMENTS

Writing a book is often a labor of love, involving many hours at the keyboard and many more hours of research, contemplation, weighing just the right way to say something, and a dash of counting ceiling tiles. But it is never accomplished alone. For this reason, Parthiv and I want to express our gratitude to friends, colleagues, and family who helped take this book from a potentially interesting idea to the pages you hold in your hand.

We want to thank the team at eLaunchers who helped keep this project on track and made meaningful contributions. We especially want to thank Dipa, Stacey, David, and Mitch. Parthiv is privileged to have a team of competent people who share his enthusiasm.

A big thank you goes out to Sue Vander Hook, an extraordinary editor, proofreader, and author of dozens of books. Sue was able to take my grammatically incorrect prose and transform it into acceptable English without going mad.

Our gratitude also goes out to Jerry and Michelle Dorris of AuthorSupport.com for their typesetting and design expertise. I find myself hiring them over and over again for each of my books, and they never disappoint. Thank you for all your wonderful work to convert a manuscript into a beautifully bound book.

We also appreciate all the input we received from Greg Banasz of Steward Partners Global Advisory. Over lunch, he provided us with valuable insights we have included in these chapters.

Tactics without strategy is the noise before defeat.

—**SunTzu,** *The Art of War*

ABOUT THE AUTHORS

Rodger A. Friedman

Rodger A. Friedman is the son a successful entrepreneur. Raised in New York City, he learned business at his father's and grandfather's knees. Rodger is a Chartered Retirement Planning Counselor^{SM}, author, Wealth Manager, and speaker with 35 years of experience providing comprehensive wealth management, retirement planning solutions, and investment strategy implementation.

Rodger is a founding partner of Steward Partners Global Advisory, an employee-owned, full-service partnership catering to family, institutional, and multigenerational investors. He leads a financial planning team based in Bethesda, Maryland.

He has authored four books on retirement planning and has been interviewed on scores of radio stations throughout the country. He has written more than a hundred articles and has been featured in *USA Today* magazine, *Fiduciary News, Fox News, FA News, Time,* and *U.S. News & World Report.* He has presented at the Author Success University Mastermind Summits and the National Publicity Summit.

Rodger is a former Senior Vice President–Wealth Management and Senior Investment Management Consultant with Morgan Stanley. He is a graduate of the State University of New York where he studied political science and economics. For the last 30 years, he has called the Washington, DC, area his home. Rodger and his wife, Reena, live in Rockville, Maryland and have two fabulous adult kids.

When asked what he does for a living, Rodger will look you in the eye and say, *"Stated plainly, our focus is to **maximize retirement clarity** to create and execute effective, efficient, and comprehensive retirement strategies for the entrepreneurial families we serve."*

Parthiv Shah

pshah@elaunchers.com

301.760.3953

To book a call with Parthiv visit www.elaunchers.com/client

> *"IMPLEMENTATION separates those who score from those who don't. It's never just what you know; it's what you do, get done, can get done by others and by automation, and can get done right consistently. Parthiv is an implementor."*
>
> **—Dan Kennedy**

Parthiv Shah is the Founder and President of eLaunchers. More than 300 dentists, physicians, and other clients from 27 states and eight countries have benefited from working with Parthiv and eLaunchers. com. He is the author of his international best-selling book *Business Kamasutra* and is a contributor to or co-author of six other books. He is co-authoring his upcoming book, *Copy That Sells*, with marketing legend Dan Kennedy. He is routinely invited to speak as a technology expert at direct marketing conferences and small group mastermind sessions.

Parthiv received his MBA in 1994. He has worked on more than 10,000 direct mail marketing projects and has mailed more than a billion pieces of direct mail. He is a veteran of the Indian Air Force, a member of the Lions Club, a *Leadership Montgomery Core Program* graduate (class of 2016), and the proud dad of an Eagle Scout.

eLaunchers was named Small Business of the Year in 2016 and inducted into the GKIC Direct Response Hall of Fame in 2017. Parthiv is a GKIC Certified Magnetic Marketing Advisor (2010), Infusionsoft Certified Partner (2011), Digital Marketer Certified Partner (2014), Click Funnels Certified Partner (2015), and HubSpot Certified Partner (2017). He is also trained on Salesforce. com, ZOHO, Microsoft Dynamics, and six other cloud-based and desktop CRM systems.

A WORD FROM PARTHIV SHAH

I want to provide some background on how Rodger and I came up with the title, *The Iceberg You Don't See*. We took a friend and colleague, Greg Banasz of Steward Partners Global Advisory, to lunch. I explained to Greg what eLaunchers and I do. I told him what a data scientist and digital marketer sees and doesn't see when first working with a client. Rodger shared about the marketing strategies he uses in his wealth management business. Rodger is a very knowledgeable direct response marketer in his financial and retirement planning practice. He shared what he sees and what *eludes him*. Together, we see the client's business from both our perspectives.

Then Greg said, "Guys, you should write a book." In succinct harmony, Rodger and I replied as if in one voice, "That's exactly what we're working on." **A special note of thanks to Greg is in order**. Thank you so much for your participation in our brainstorming session. Your contributions are extremely appreciated. The success of our efforts could not have been so insightful without your support and encouragement.

So why did we decide on the metaphor of an <u>iceberg</u> and why should you adopt it in your own financial advisory practice?

<u>An iceberg is only partially visible.</u> The portion you see above the water is menacing when sailing directly at it. It's even impressive from a distance, but we know it can be disastrous should we strike it with, say, a ship. The part we don't see is where the real danger lies; it's under water where the mass of this floating glacier resides.

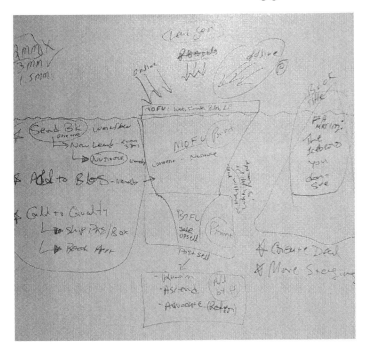

Hopefully, your ship—your financial advisor practice—is equipped with the wherewithal to avoid danger. Your clients understand the inherent risks, but they expect you to handle the assets they have entrusted to your care with kid gloves and without incident.

Know this in advance of your possible *Titanic* moments: Icebergs *are* floating in your seas, and the parts you don't see can and will sink you. They're unavoidable. Market downturns, recessions, rising interest rates, deflation—the threats are real, and the threats are numerous. There's at least one with your name on it. It's your destiny. Icebergs are part of everyone's life. But you still have choices.

Rest assured, by the end of this book, you will have the route to your destination all mapped out. Icebergs are only water, albeit rock-solid, frozen water. You can sail straight into them, or you can sail around them. Choose wisely.

A WORD FROM RODGER A. FRIEDMAN

The fact that you are reading this book indicates that you are interested in **growing your practice and your revenues**.

And that pushes you to the front of the line, past all those <u>who do nothing</u> to propel their businesses to the next level.

I have spent the last six years learning marketing strategies, something I was never taught at Hutton, Shearson, Smith Barney, or Morgan Stanley. I've attended many conferences, learned from marketing superheroes, and taken enough notes to wallpaper my garage.

I learned the power of authoring my own books—this is my fifth—something that resonated with me. I came to understand the power of a sales letter, something I had no clue was important, although I had received sales letters from businesses for years.

I met and became friends with *master copywriters* and *direct marketing experts*. Truth be told, I didn't know that was even a *thing* until I learned that a series of letters crafted by one of these experts could generate $2 million and more in revenue. I was astounded! These were cash-in-the-bank multimillionaires whose *work* was to write sales letters.

A whole new world of marketing opened up to me as if a curtain had been lifted, revealing secret marketing strategies I never knew existed. Like you, the only financial advisor marketing I was aware of was the brochures created by corporate marketing departments, and they never seemed like they were worth the *investment*.

I invite you to take in every word of this book and all the years of wisdom contained in it. *Financial Advisor Marketing* is the result of dozens of plane flights, numerous conferences, untold nights in Marriott's and Hiltons, hours of note taking, and years of reading scores of books by the likes of Dan Kennedy, Jay Abraham, Gary Halbert, John Carlton, Doberman Dan, Joe Polish, Tommy Hopkins and others.

I invite you to learn what I've learned! Benefit from my experiences! Harvest what I've already planted! And then grow your own practice and increase your revenues!

TABLE OF CONTENTS

Introduction   *xxi*

Part I: Secrets of Financial Advisor Marketing That Firms Don't Teach

CHAPTER 1   Marketing Your Practice   3
What Differentiates You?

CHAPTER 2   Financial Advisor Marketing   11
The Prospects, the Strategy, the Potential

CHAPTER 3   My Path of Discovery   21
The Business of Marketing

CHAPTER 4   Common Marketing Assumptions and Mistakes   25
Exposing Financial Advisor Marketing Myths

CHAPTER 5   Four Obstacles to Marketing   35
The Ones That Are Extremely Difficult to Overcome

CHAPTER 6   How Firms View Financial Advisor Marketing   41
Say Hello to Your Corporate Marketing Department

CHAPTER 7   Own Your Own Media   51
Have You Ever Thought about That?

CHAPTER 8   What I Learned from Other Professions   55
Some Essentials to Understand

CHAPTER 9   Authority Marketing   63
               Separating Yourself from the Competition

CHAPTER 10 The Architecture of Authority   69
               Who Knows More about You Than You?

CHAPTER 11 The Essential Element of Any Financial   79
               Advisory Practice
               Growth

CHAPTER 12 Five Mistakes of a Financial Advisor   85
               How Not to Market Your Practice

CHAPTER 13 Innovative Marketing Ideas   91
               The High-End Aluminum Briefcase

CHAPTER 14 A Failure to Survive   99
               *Make Marketing the Lifeblood of
               Your Practice*

CHAPTER 15 My $250,000 Aha Moment   105
               Where to Spend Your Money

CHAPTER 16 Marketing Assessment   111
               How Am I Doing?

CHAPTER 17 An Unlikely Pair   117
               *The Merger of Financial Advising and
               Tech Marketing*

Part II: The Iceberg You Don't See
Art and Science of Marketing Mechanics

CHAPTER 18 The Importance of Systems, Processes,   123
               and Rhythms
               What Separates Good from Great?

CHAPTER 19 Why We Compare Your Marketing and   131
               Sales to an Iceberg
               Is Your Business Titanic II?

CHAPTER 20 The Top of the Iceberg   137
               Everything Visible

CHAPTER 21   The Top of The Funnel (TOFU)   147
Your Internal Marketing Efforts

CHAPTER 22   The Middle of The Funnel (MOFU)   157
Identifying Your External Market

CHAPTER 23   The Bottom of the Funnel (BOFU)   167
When Your Prospect Reaches the Bottom

Part III: eLaunchers' Tools for Effective Marketing Product and Service Offerings

CHAPTER 24   eLaunchers' Tools for   173
Effective Marketing
Product and Service Offerings

eLaunchers' Private Client   177
Monthly Services

Success Blueprint   181

Done for You – High-Value Client   189
Marketing Machine

eLaunchers' Smart Start New Lead   193
Development Program

eLaunchers' Direct-   197
Connect HANDWRITTEN

The Ultimate Gift from Parthiv   201
and Rodger

Introduction

RODGER A. FRIEDMAN

*In any oversaturated environment, it doesn't matter how wonderful you are and how much you have to offer. If your message fails to fascinate, you've failed....**Being the best isn't enough, if nobody notices or cares.***

—**Sally Hogshead**
Author, *Fascinate: Your 7 Triggers to Persuasion and Captivation*

COUNTLESS FINANCIAL ADVISORS have **never been taught how to effectively market their professional practices.** They were trained in financial planning and a wide variety of investments, including stocks, bonds, mutual funds, estate planning, debt, asset allocation, retirement planning, taxation, and more.

But most were never taught **marketing—the part of the "iceberg" they don't see** and the **key to growing their business.**

Many are **woefully unaware of how big and how important marketing is,** and they work to grow their client base and revenues without a well thought out strategic framework.

So what *is* the right strategic marketing framework? How do financial advisors effectively market their practices? It starts with knowing *who you are*.

WHO ARE YOU?

Any financial advisor can run a financial planning business. You don't need to be certified, registered, or chartered to create a 125-page report. And you can use any binder or notebook to organize the numerous sections, charts, and spreadsheets in that report. Yes, you are a financial advisor, but **who are you**...really?

> *Cerulli Associates estimates that there are 300,000 financial advisors in the United States.*

> **How are you different than the other 299,999?**

Let's assume you are competent, that you can assemble a comprehensive financial planning report, and that you are not mystified by the software. So what is the variable element here? It's *you*—not the report.

> **You see, beyond a certain point, you are paid for who you are, not for what you produce.**

Now read that sentence again.

What do you charge for a 125-page financial plan? $1,925? Perhaps $6,500? What would it take for your financial plan to be priced at $14,000 or more? Remember this: What you charge has more to do with **who you are** than the 125-page report.

Let's look at an example. Take a family doctor or general practitioner who has an annual income of $285,000. Compare that doctor to a specialist, an ophthalmologist, who makes $680,000 per year. Or perhaps an ophthalmologist to the stars. And maybe that ophthalmologist has authored three books on LASIK surgery, has appeared on radio and TV interviews, and brings home more than $2.4 million per year. That ophthalmologist is definitely a successful specialist—as well as a **celebrity**.

All these physicians have invested about the same amount of time in medical school, and they all are practicing medicine full time. But the doctor who is a celebrity out-earns the general practitioner more than eight times. Is that celebrity doctor eight times smarter? Did that doctor attend medical school eight times longer? The answers are most likely no. So what is the difference?

Here's what Dan Kennedy teaches. The specialist—the **celebrity**—is a <u>more important *who*</u> in the marketplace. **People are willing to pay more** for those who are certified, have a specialty, and are famous in their niche.

You're probably thinking that this applies only to top doctors. Wrong! It applies to virtually every field or job. So let me ask you this:

- *Who* are you in your field?
- *What* is your specialty?
- *Where* are you looking for prospects?
- *When* are you going to make yourself known through unique marketing strategies?

◆ *How* will you set yourself apart from the other 299,999 financial advisors?

WHO AM I?

I am Rodger Friedman, a financial advisor, but I am also the son of a dry cleaner. Early in my career as a financial advisor, I focused my marketing on owners of dry cleaning stores because I knew their problems and concerns inside and out. I understood their challenges and had experience in their *niche* because I had spent years behind the mammoth dry cleaning machine in my dad's store. And I *knew* how my dad and his friends invested.

I focused my practice on bearer bonds. For those not old enough to remember, owners cut off interest coupons, took them to the bank, and exchanged them for cash—tax-free cash. This conservative type of investment resonated with owners of dry cleaning stores. I didn't show up at a financial planning meeting with a 25-slide PowerPoint presentation. All I needed was a pencil and the back of a napkin. It was a simple concept that prospects understood quickly.

I also found that many dry cleaning store owners talked to each other, and some of them recommended me to other owners. Some asked me to speak at association meetings, and **I became well known in my niche**. Referrals were easy. I became *"famous"* in their world. I wouldn't call myself a celebrity, but folks knew my name. They welcomed my calls and didn't see me as an intrusion.

Here are some questions you may want to ask yourself:

◆ Do you serve a niche?
◆ Are you welcomed in your niche?
◆ Are you a celebrity or well known in your niche?

- Have you spoken at association meetings for your niche?
- Have you been interviewed on radio or TV?
- Have you written special reports on your area of expertise?
- Have you written a book—or two or three or five?

Do you suppose any of these points might make you an ***important who*** in the field of financial advising? Would any of these set you apart as a ***specialist***? Would any of these give you access to ***high-caliber prospects*** whose portfolios would allow you to charge more than $14,000 for a 125-page financial plan? The answer to all these questions is a resounding *yes*!

> *So how do you do it? How do you set yourself apart?*
> *How do you create a specialty and a marketing*
> *strategy that are unique to you?*

Come with me on this journey. Let's walk through this book and find out ***which financial advisor you are***. Let's learn how to strategically market the ***Who*** (you), not the ***What*** (that 125-page report), and maybe even end up with a ***7-figure income*** (yes, I said 7)!

—Rodger Friedman

PART I

Marketing for Financial Advisors: The Iceberg You Don't See

SECRETS OF FINANCIAL ADVISOR MARKETING THAT FIRMS DON'T TEACH

Marketing
Your Practice

. . . .

What Differentiates You?

If you want to leap-frog to a much higher income, then you must master marketing of yourself, use a more sophisticated approach to your business and your work with customers and focus on learning the strategies that are proven to catapult wealth.

—Dan Kennedy

THE INCOME POTENTIAL of an advisor is virtually *unlimited*—an idea that a sizable number of advisors haven't considered. Very few planners or advisors are paid on an hourly basis, and they appear to be unaware of the entrepreneurial mandate inherent in their chosen profession.

In a way, the average financial planner or advisor is *no different* than any other professional such as a dentist or chiropractor who has the appropriate credentials but little or no growth in revenues or patient count. These professionals most likely completed a curriculum that did not include intelligent marketing strategies or methods for growing their practices. Many professionals are technically proficient at their craft but lack the knowledge of how to get patents or clients in the door. They are totally ignorant about how to do that.

Have you ever caught yourself thinking, *I'm very good at what I do, but I could be doing better*? Achieving maximum success in your business is often tied to **effective marketing practices**.

Many professionals focus on their trade, becoming better at their core deliverables, more technically proficient at the *doing*. While this is vitally important, many do not see past it. Just as essential is the awareness of key activities that *must* be undertaken to grow a practice. This is an area that many planners and advisors don't spend enough time on. A common assumption is that market returns will *naturally* increase revenues. Marketing to increase the profits of a practice becomes an afterthought.

Consider two dentists, one filling cavities all day for $225 each and another who specializes in implants for $3,700 per patient. The first dentist has never clearly identified the profile of the patients he serves best. He believes that *everyone has teeth and cavities and thus everyone is his potential patient*. The dentist performing implants all day has a very specific idea of who her most enjoyable and profitable patients are and relentlessly markets to them. With this in mind, our hypothetical *implant dentist* seeks out only ideal prospects and uses multiple methods to attract them to her practice. She understands that the success of her practice is predicated on the success of her marketing. The *all-day cavity dentist* is oblivious to intelligent marketing strategies that can be used to grow his practice.

Circling back to the financial services industry, many advisors don't have a clear concept of **who their best clients are.** Often, their book of business reads like the yellow pages: electricians, restaurant owners, teachers, pharmacists, builders, and so on. If they were asked to build a profile or an avatar of their perfect client, many would find it difficult and would default to overused terms such as *the affluent* or *the mass affluent.* They may be aware that their average client is married, has kids, and is a homeowner, but that's about it.

A MORE IMPORTANT "WHO"

Take a look at your client list. Now take a look at you and your practice. Are you the same as any other planner or financial advisor? Is there any difference between you and the thousands of others out there? How do your clients, prospects, and target audience see you?

What differentiates you and your practice in the eyes of a prospect? Is it your credentials or your financial planning process? Maybe it's your team structure—unless you are a solo operator, which carries its own set of negative perceptions and challenges.

Dan Kennedy teaches that as you go up the ladder of income, **you are paid more for who you are than what you do.** In other words, what are you doing to make yourself <u>a more important **who**</u>? Have you created authority? Are you a celebrity within a niche?

Just because you hang out a shingle telling the world you are in business does not mean you will run a successful and growing practice. Ask any dentist or chiropractor, and they will tell you the same thing. You need to separate yourself from the pack. That does not necessarily mean you are better than your competitors, but it does mean *you are perceived differently*.

Consider the cost of a financial plan completed by Suze Orman, financial planning guru and media star, versus a plan offered by an advisor along route 59 in Lawrence, Kansas. My belief is that Orman's plan would cost multiples more than a plan completed by our hypothetical Kansas advisor. **Why?** Because she has made herself **a more important** *who*.

The ability to separate yourself from the competition has everything to do with **how** you are perceived by your target market and what **tools** you use to market yourself.

You achieve this through a *complex and multidimensional marketing strategy*.

Perhaps you have noticed an advisor in your city or town who has already taken this to heart. That advisor is generally the one with a growing practice and the one other advisors despise. Perhaps you have noticed the following about those types of advisors:

- They have a billboard ad along the highway
- Their message and photo adorn the backs of buses as well as bus stop shelters
- They have their own financial radio show
- They are active in a local charity
- They give away free copies of their retirement planning books
- They sponsor the Little League team
- They use direct mail
- They are an officer in the local Chamber of Commerce
- They host retirement planning dinners at the local Holiday Inn

♦ They have a monthly newsletter that they mail to all their
clients and prospects

♦ They cultivate centers of influence such as CPAs
and attorneys

That advisor has taken many steps to be visible. And it is NOT an accident. It is strategic; it is a product of a complex marketing strategy to **increase awareness** in that advisor's target market. It is something that **differentiates** that advisor from all the other advisors.

DIFFERENTIATE YOURSELF

So how do you differentiate yourself—separate yourself from the legions of other advisors?

Sally Hogshead, National Speakers Association Hall of Fame speaker and *New York Times* bestselling author of **Fascinate: How to Make Your Brand Impossible to Resist**, focuses on the central theme that you do not have to be better than everyone else—just different. She goes on to say, "Fascination is the most powerful force of attraction, drawing customers into a state of intense focus."

So I pose this question to you: **What differentiates you and your practice?** Do you provide overwhelming value to your clients? Are you an influencer? Have you created a *complex process* that takes prospects and clients through a comprehensive checklist of crucial issues? Do you fascinate your clients or prospects? Do you hold them in a state of intense focus, or do you bore them with financial speak?

I have met advisors who have a complex process, and I have met advisors who think they can *wing it* with each new prospect. Which financial advisor are you? Do you guide prospective clients through a series of discovery sessions that unearth important family issues? Do you inspire them with <u>stories</u> of successful planning outcomes and alert them to potential financial disasters? Do you use emotion to keep your prospects focused on the most important challenges they will face? Do you make the financial planning process **personal**?

THE ACE FORMULA

Let's break it down to a formula—the **ACE Formula**—*Authority, Celebrity, Expertise.* This concept is central to creating differentiation in your advisory practice.

We've already talked about **celebrity**—the *important you*. Clients want to know that you are somebody. Potential clients want to know they are dealing with someone who has experience working with families like theirs. And then there's credibility. <u>How do you create credibility in the eyes of your prospects and clients</u>? If you are perceived as lacking credibility, your chances of winning important new clients will be severely impacted. And when you have credibility, you will cultivate **authority** on a foundation of **expertise**.

AUTHORITY MAY BE GENERATED BY *WHAT YOU HAVE DONE*

- ◆ What past achievements speak to your credibility?
- ◆ Have you won any awards or received credentials or advanced designations?
- ◆ What activities have you engaged in?
- ◆ Have you held a series of financial planning seminars in your town?
- ◆ Have you taught financial planning at the local college?
- ◆ Have you been interviewed by newspapers or magazines?

♦ Have you been interviewed by local radio or TV stations?

♦ Have you written any books to showcase your expertise?

If I have successfully grabbed your attention, you now understand that you can be **somebody**, and you can **purposely and deliberately manufacture <u>authority</u>**. As you gain authority and credibility, you are more likely to attract higher-caliber clients.

Successful clients prefer dealing with **successful advisors**. How do you think your prospects might react if they received an auto-graphed, personalized copy of a book you authored prior to sitting down with you? <u>How do you showcase your success?</u> If your answer is the production awards hanging on your office wall, I have one rec-ommendation. Take them down—NOW.

Replace them with **you**—a financial advisor with deliberately manufactured authority, a high level of celebrity, and, of course, expertise. Then go after your chosen clients with an **effective, stra-tegic marketing plan**.

Financial Advisor Marketing

......

The Prospects,
the Strategy, the Potential

A comfort zone is a beautiful place...but nothing grows there.

—**Unknown**

RELATIVELY FEW FINANCIAL advisors are able to clearly identify the profile of the client they serve best. Here are some examples of client profiles:

◆ Women ages 45 to 60
◆ Single, divorced, or widowed
◆ Have no kids
◆ Small business owners, primarily retail stores
◆ Live in suburban locations

♦ Worried if they will ever be able to retire

Or perhaps something like this:

♦ Corporate executives at publicly traded companies
♦ Conservative politically
♦ Ages 50 to 62
♦ Hold stock options
♦ Kids heading to college
♦ Non-working spouse
♦ Homeowner

Whoever your *clients* are and the more you know about them, the more likely *you will market them* with effectiveness and success. You would not market to an attorney the same way you would market to a brick manufacturer. You would not market to an engineer the same way you would market to someone who owns a chain of yogurt stores. **Unfortunately, most marketing materials available to advisors today treat all prospects exactly the same way.**

A valuable exercise may be to build a spreadsheet of all your clients and focus on their occupations and how profitable they are to your practice. You may also want to rate how much you enjoy working with them and if they provide referrals. When you're done, ask yourself these questions:

♦ Are there any concentrations in one, two, or three industries?
♦ Does any occupation stand out to you as being very profitable?
♦ Does any occupation stand out as a pain in the neck?
♦ Does any occupation stand out as having low profitability?

◆ If you were to clone your best clients, what industries would they be in?

◆ What other commonalities can you identify?

While I won't spend a lot of time segmenting your book of business, understand that in the pursuit of prospects, you may want to market to each occupation a bit differently. As I mentioned previously, you will talk to an engineer differently than someone who owns a retail store.

Being a highly effective marketer of your services is a valuable skill that most advisors won't take the time to master. Yet they will take the time to increase the letters after their name by adding additional certifications. (Think of the professor of human sexuality who lives alone and never dates.) In many cases, they would be better off increasing their knowledge of marketing.

I DON'T KNOW WHAT TO DO

A major obstacle to effective financial advisor marketing is that many FAs ***don't know what to do***. They know that marketing is a good idea and that they should do it, but the idea often stops there. The problem is frequently one of confusion and decision paralysis.

Many advisors and planners believe that building a practice mirrors the Kevin Costner movie *Field of Dreams*. He built a baseball diamond in the middle of an Iowa cornfield and relied on the promise to *"build it and they will come."* And financial advisors can't expect guaranteed success if they simply obtain a credential, hang up a shingle, announce to the world that they are open for business, and hope people come. In the absence of effective marketing, a whole bunch of time, effort, and money may have just been wasted.

Browse the cereal aisle in the local grocery store, and you'll be confronted with hundreds of choices for breakfast cereals. Old standbys such as Captain Crunch and Cheerios now come in six different varieties. Most of us grew up with just one. We never had to tell mom *which one* we wanted.

Likewise, many financial advisors are confused and uncertain about marketing because there are **so many options to choose from**, and the potential costs could skyrocket. Add to that the time and effort involved, and FAs would much rather take the easy route and take a *done-for-you approach*.

Often I hear, *"Well, we are working on a brochure."* Odds are that the brochure will end up looking like the corporate marketing department designed it. The basics will be there—who you are, what you do, and a bio of each team member. But it's not exactly a compelling piece of copy. Advisors will also most likely spend too much money making the brochure *look professional* and will print too many copies that will just sit on your shelf.

But here's the ugly truth. **Most FAs default to no marketing at all.** When asked how they get new clients, the stock answer is *referrals*. And there is rarely a referral system in place. And truth be told, the number of referrals is very small.

Many advisors are content doing practically nothing to grow their business, with the occasional six- or seven-figure rollover or referral providing incremental growth. But even that does not guarantee growth.

And as we are all painfully aware, long-time clients pass away. Their beneficiaries and heirs often transfer the funds, regardless of how close a relationship you had with the deceased.

But have you thought about ***intergenerational marketing***? If you worked through a plan before your client passed away, you might be able to continue advising and managing assets for the beneficiaries. In our practice, we have a high degree of success maintaining relationships with family members of deceased clients. We cultivate relationships with beneficiaries and add them to our *marketing funnels* so we are constantly in front of them.

You might be saying, **but I don't have any education in marketing**. There are many effective approaches to growing your practice that do not require a PhD in marketing. But keep in mind that whatever method you choose will have a learning curve, and you will need to study it before implementing it. Make sure you understand each aspect of your strategy and that nothing is left to chance. <u>You will want to get it right the first time, so don't just choose a random strategy and see how it works.</u> Though not a perfect analogy, I would not want to start using a 45-caliber handgun just to *see how it works*.

MARKETING YOURSELF

Before we go further, I would like to define a term. The word is **COPY**. According to Wikipedia, copy is "written content that aims to increase brand awareness and ultimately persuade a person or group to take a particular action."

Whenever you look at brochures, pamphlets, and white papers produced by your firm's marketing department, you are looking at *copy* written by folks in the marketing department. And the average marketing associate at your firm does not know much about your personal business. I would suggest that after doing some research and studying some advertising methods, you produce some decent copy yourself.

If we were to examine the normal day of a financial advisor, we might find the following typical activities: client meetings, client calls, operational matters, investment research, creating financial plans, and perhaps some prospecting. It's easy to see what is missing. Seldom are *marketing activities* part of the average day. Advisors are so wrapped up <u>working *in* their business</u> that they don't block out time to <u>work *on* their business</u>.

If financial advisors were asked what they want their business to look like in three years or five years (how many new clients, revenues, assets under management, etc.), most would not be able to articulate their plan. Some might provide tentative numbers, but when pushed on how they will generate new business, they would probably look like a deer in the headlights and give the stock answer: referrals.

So let's get uncomfortable for a minute: No doubt you have attended dozens of investment conferences over your career, as I have. Have you ever attended a marketing conference that focuses on methods of growing your practice and increasing revenues? Most would answer no. What about you?

When it comes to marketing, financial advisors are often their own worst enemies. What do I mean by that? Well, how about the following:

◆ **Many FAs have no idea what effective and successful marketing is.** A well designed and effective marketing system has the ability to deliver a steady stream of prospects predisposed to sitting down with you. The important point is that you want to *develop a marketing system*, not a one-and-done project. A wide variety of professionals are available to assist you in crafting and refining a system that makes sense for you *and* implementing it in your practice.

♦ **Countless FAs are unaware of the concept of building marketing assets.** They were trained in financial planning and investments, not building and growing a business. So, you may ask, why is a marketing asset important? A marketing asset is a **system** that can continually provide prospects to your practice, month after month, year after year. It's kind of like a machine that produces prospects. I have met professionals who have been using the same *direct mail* letter sequence with minor changes for more than five years. They **invested in a marketing asset** that has produced increased clients and revenues for years.

♦ **Many FAs find it difficult to separate marketing opinions and assumptions from facts.** Advisors have told me that a strategy doesn't work because a colleague reported poor results. Face it, advisors are not known as marketing experts. Often, advisors' ideas of marketing are based on hearsay rather than firsthand knowledge.

♦ Often, **an FA's concept of marketing is a Social Security seminar** at a local hotel or restaurant featuring a chicken dinner and a PowerPoint presentation, paid for and presented by an insurance company or mutual fund representative.

♦ **FAs seldom view themselves as an owner of their practice.** They believe they are an employee of a larger firm or a broker dealer. They lack an owner's mentality—they <u>don't view themselves</u> as in charge of their own practice. Rarely do FAs internalize the idea that their income potential is limitless, constrained only by their ability to *outmarket the competition*. I have also met advisors who have embraced intelligent marketing solutions and supercharged the revenue growth of their practices.

♦ **Many FAs have established a pattern where <u>actual marketing</u> is the exception and not a primary function of their practices.** They fail to *block out time* to work solely on marketing strategies. After speaking with hundreds of advisors to research ideas for this book, I came to the conclusion that a large number of the advisors I spoke with spent less than one hour a week in marketing. The number of advisors committed to a marketing system was negligible.

♦ **FAs, if they market at all, focus solely on one means of marketing,** one means of attracting prospective clients. Keep in mind that you want to present many *open doors* for prospects to walk through and discover you. Direct mail, newsletters, blogs, radio interviews, bring-a-friend gatherings, books, special reports, quizzes, referrals from centers of influence, and assessments are only some of the resources available to you.

The above points are not an exaggeration. I have seen advisors mail a one-time, pre-printed, off-the-shelf, product-focused 3x5 inch postcard to a purchased prospect list with virtually no results. Little thought went into the list selection. So they decided that *postcards don't work*. It's not rocket science to understand that if you put practically no effort into a project, you will likely see little results.

Also, remember that not everything works well the first time. Ideas often need to be examined further and refined so the results will improve.

Marketing is not a small issue. Its implications for your practice are enormous. While there are many strategies for effective marketing, I firmly believe that you get what you pay for. Seeking asset managers for ideas might be a good alternative, although it may come with strings attached and the expectation of steering future business their way. Financial advisors around the country have sought out my guidance on these matters, but I have agreed to coach only a limited number of them on ways to improve or implement effective marketing systems.

Consider the advisor who writes a book called *The Seven Deadly Sins of Retirement Investing* and then mails oversized postcards with a compelling message to members of his or her church. Emblazoned on the card is this message: **May I Send You a Free Copy of My New Book?** The advisor repeats the same process for members of a service organization, the local Chamber of Commerce, and so on. The results? Incredible!

*If there is any part of your business that **should** be systemized, it is the marketing of your business.*

My Path of Discovery

The Business of Marketing

Look at what the majority of people are doing, and do the exact opposite, and you'll probably never go wrong for as long as you live.

—Earl Nightingale

IN THE SPRING of 2013, my wife, kids, and I loaded up the car and drove to Cape Cod to enjoy a week with my sister and brother-in-law at their home. The waterfront house had a dock and a boat, which would provide hours of family enjoyment. Prior to our trip, I starting reading business development and marketing books, searching for ideas to expand the revenues of my practice. Although I ran a good business, there was definitely room for improvement, as well as more high-value clients.

As I plowed through half a dozen books, I kept seeing one name—*Dan Kennedy*—pop up time and time again. You don't have to hit me on the head with a brick. If all these authors were referencing the same guy, I wanted to know why.

I easily found him on Amazon since he had authored more than 14 books on marketing. Evidently, he helped thousands of entrepreneurs earn millions of dollars in a wide variety of businesses. I felt like a kid in a candy store as I chose two attention-grabbing titles in the *NO BS* series to bring on my Cape Cod trip.

While my wife and kids were off shopping, I took one of the books down to the dock, hopped in the boat, and sat there and read. I was captivated. Kennedy spoke in a strange, new language that was spellbinding. He made so much sense and drilled down into concepts I had never considered. He introduced me to unknown marketing concepts I could use to grow my practice. I dog-eared many pages that day, finishing the entire book while gently rocking in the boat. The next day, I read the second book. I was officially hooked on his marketing concepts and business philosophy.

While I was comfortable earning a six-figure income as a financial advisor, I probably focused on marketing only one hour each month. Thinking back, I'm amazed that I was able to grow my business at all, considering my feeble attempts at marketing. And in those days, I was not aware of anyone in my branch office who spent any significant amount of time on marketing.

I took advantage of an offer in each of Kennedy's books and signed up for an inexpensive membership in his marketing organization. I learned some marketing strategies and quickly found out they were applicable to nearly all businesses, not just financial advisors. It seems I was learning tactics used successfully by dentists, plastic surgeons, lawn care companies, carpet cleaners, chiropractors, lawyers, and others.

Then I attended one of Kennedy's conferences. I heard him say **two things** that changed my view of business.

FIRST

I must embrace the reality that for maximum income, I must be in *the business of marketing*, and I must effectively translate, creatively develop, and wisely transfer best strategies and examples from any place they occur, from any business, to mine. In short, I must think differently in order to grow rich.

SECOND

You can *never delegate the marketing of your business*. You can make more money marketing your business than any other business-related activity.

I spent massive amounts of time combing through Kennedy's books, extracting key ideas and writing them in my journals. I filled six good-sized notebooks with Kennedy's marketing strategies, tactics, and philosophy. I was convinced this was a better use of my time than reading dozens of science fiction books.

My big payoff came as I implemented the ideas I had placed in my journals and saw my business and revenues expand. I knew I was on the right path when other advisors thought I was weird, doing things they and others did not do.

If I was going to leap-frog my income, I had to abandon the methods I was taught and adopt the philosophy that I must be my own director of marketing. The marketing department at my broker dealer had nothing even remotely as useful as what I was learning.

I started to learn and internalize what I was reading. Slowly, I began to implement some of the concepts I was exposed to. I was spending more and more time marketing my business. Within six months, I saw significant results. Within a year, I experienced meaningful increases in revenues. I was hooked.

I signed up for additional conferences throughout the country. It didn't matter where Kennedy was speaking. I just got on a plane, booked the hotel, and went. Dallas, Chicago, Denver, Orlando—wherever he was, I was going. I was *all in*. I met my co-author, Parthiv Shah, at one of those conferences. He stumbled across Kennedy a few years before I did, and I quickly saw that he was a master at implementing these strategies.

I quickly realized my broker dealer's view of marketing was of limited value to me in growing my practice. I also realized that if I engaged in the normal type of marketing that other advisors practice, I would receive the ordinary and average results they receive.

So how was I going to start marketing right? How would I get past **ordinary** marketing and create an **extraordinary** marketing strategy with much more than average results? And then I have to ask you this: ***How will you do this?***

First, we need to bust some **marketing myths**—some common marketing assumptions and mistakes.

Common Marketing Assumptions and Mistakes

. . . .

Busting Financial Advisor Marketing Myths

Everything you were taught about marketing is wrong.

—Unknown

THE FIRST STEP in mastering a marketing strategy is getting rid of marketing myths. Most assumptions financial advisors make about marketing their business are false, and a lot of opportunities are lost due to these misguided beliefs.

Let's look at nine myths most FAs believe—nine myths that need to be busted so their practices can grow.

1. THAT WON'T WORK FOR ME BECAUSE MY BUSINESS IS DIFFERENT.

Many advisors and planners falsely believe that their only marketing options are what their firms make available to them. It's usually an array of pamphlets, brochures, and white papers. If something interesting or unique catches advisors' eyes, perhaps something from a mattress store or a chiropractor's office, they dismiss it with this thought: **That won't work for me because my business is different**.

What many don't realize is that <u>no business is different</u>. The goal of all businesses is to acquire new clients and keep them for a long time. It's the same with the medical profession: acquire new patients and keep them for a long time. The goal of an advisor's business is to acquire clients and, you guessed it, keep them for a long time!

Let's translate that into some numbers you can wrap your head around.

A $2,500,000 client at an annual consulting and management fee of 1.15% is $28,750 the first year plus a $12,500 financial planning fee. That totals more than $155,000 in revenues over five years. Over 10 years, the client generates fees of more than $300,000.

Your objective should be to gain a competitive advantage by studying business and marketing <u>outside the financial services industry</u>. *Innovation often comes from taking something in one industry and applying it to another.*

2. DIRECT RESPONSE MAIL DOESN'T WORK IN MY BUSINESS.

Think back to the advisor who sent preprinted, product-oriented 3x5 postcards to a purchased list. Odds are that the one-time exercise produced poor results. Had the advisor had a bit more imagination, he or she might have brainstormed a multi-step sequence that was not a product pitch but a more personal message delivered to a specific audience.

The advisor might have used **multiple media methods** to deliver the message over a period of time. That may have included writing a sales letter, having it approved by the compliance folks, and then delivering the message in different ways, such as a letter or an oversized postcard.

Central to this idea is that the communication contains a compelling offer. Whether the offer is a free white paper, a personalized Social Security evaluation, or a free 50-minute retirement consultation, the offer must be clear, concise, and compelling, and have a deadline for a response.

Whether you ultimately decide that your marketing sequence should have three steps, seven steps, or 12 steps, your most important decision is to take action and execute. You can *never* wait for the time to be *just right* because it will never be just right.

3. DIRECT RESPONSE MAIL DOESN'T WORK IN MY TOWN.

The specifics of how a direct response mail project might be structured can be as different as night and day. But the idea that it works in North Carolina but *not* in South Carolina is ridiculous. Equally as ridiculous is that it works in Scarsdale but not Hartsdale. Direct mail works when it is properly structured with a persuasive message and a compelling offer delivered to the right audience. Absent any of those elements, the project most likely will fail.

Here's a message that is neither persuasive nor compelling and is likely to fail:

Hi, I'm Joe the CFP®, and I opened an office next to the UPS store at the corner of 5th and Main. Drop by for details about our exciting new financial planning process.

4. THERE AREN'T ANY CREATIVE MARKETING CONCEPTS OUT THERE.

For your marketing message to be delivered *and opened* by the right prospects, you may need to use your imagination. Why? If your prospect has a seven-figure net worth, odds are you are not the only one in town vying for his or her attention. You are often competing with the hardware store, the dry cleaner, the insurance agent, the real estate agent, the local dentist, and other financial advisors. Your message needs to be different. Notice that I didn't say *better*; I said *different*.

I met one advisor who shipped a full-sized canoe paddle to a select group of prospects with this message: *If your financial advisor left you up a creek without a paddle, here's a paddle.* Laugh all you like, but the strategy worked like a charm and produced many prospect meetings. The point is, the advisor did something different and was *noticed in a sea of advertising sameness.*

What if you delivered your message in some unusual way? Perhaps in neon bright green envelopes or in a replica of a bank cash deposit bag. Do they sound far-fetched? Think again. I know multi-million-dollar businesses that are prospecting in these exact ways and are making millions.

I have seen successful direct response marketing sequences delivered in a replica of a trash can with a message that reads, *Since you keep throwing out my messages, I thought I would give you a trash can!* And, in case you were wondering, the Post Office delivered all the messages, even the garbage cans. You might think some of these strategies are odd or bizarre, but people notice them. Unusual, different, and even ugly messages get noticed.

The late Gary Halbert, perhaps the most talented direct response copywriter on the planet, would tell his conference attendees that most Americans sort their mail over the garbage pail. The A pile is for bills, correspondence from friends and family, and important items to read. The B pile is for magazines they subscribe to and items they want to read at a later date. The C pile is mail that doesn't even get read and goes straight to the garbage can. Your goal, he would say, is to end up on the A pile.

Unusual marketing ideas share one very important characteristic. Prospects open the messages and respond to the offers. Millions of dollars are being made with non-traditional messages delivered in non-traditional ways. Here is the point: these marketers showed up like nobody else and got noticed; and people read their messages instead of putting them in the C pile.

I'm not suggesting that you put a message in a trash can or colored envelope, although that may improve your marketing response rate. I'm showing you that there is a world of marketing outside of the staid, corporate, and formal marketing department messages you are familiar with. If you think your options for marketing your practice are limited, you're right. If you think your options for marketing your practice are unlimited, you're also right!

For a graduate-level crash course in marketing, I suggest you read

Dan Kennedy's book *Magnetic Marketing: How to Attract a Flood of New Customers That Pay, Stay, and Refer*. For a free copy, send a request to my co-author, Parthiv Shah.

5. MY CLIENTS ARE TOO SOPHISTICATED FOR MARKETING GIMMICKS.

Walk into a corporate executive's office and you might find his or her 8th grade soccer trophy or first place plaque for the bass fishing competition. All our prospects and clients are human with emotions, wants, and desires.

People make purchase decisions largely based on emotional reasons and backed up with logic. Whether the purchase is a computer system, a backhoe, or the services of a financial planner, human nature is at work, no matter how sophisticated a prospect.

I recall a story Dan Kennedy told me. He was attending a lunch meeting years ago with the recently deceased Lee Iacocca, who paid for the group's pizzas with carefully folded discount coupons that were tucked away in his wallet.

Iacocca was the son of Italian immigrants who settled in Allentown, Pennsylvania. His dad held a variety of jobs, including a cobbler and a restaurant owner, and taught his son the value of money. Even after years as the chief executive of Chrysler, Iacocca's internal wiring *held firm* despite a net worth of many millions of dollars.

One could argue that the chairman and chief executive of one of America's largest car companies was a sophisticated consumer who made decisions solely based on logic. They would be wrong. Everyone is influenced by their upbringing and environment. Remember, as you consider marketing strategies, you are marketing to people with emotions, no matter how sophisticated you think they are. The buying emotion and the buying process are the same. When it comes to marketing messages, emotions trump logic. Remember that.

6. ADDING ANOTHER CREDENTIAL TO MY NAME IS MORE IMPORTANT THAN MARKETING.

Many advisors believe that if they are *good at what they do*, clients and centers of influence will rush to refer others to them. Unfortunately, technical competence does not guarantee a healthy stream of referrals. Truth be told, if someone hires a financial planner to complete a plan, they <u>expect</u> the planner to be good. That is a baseline requirement—they are good at what they do. If I go into an auto repair shop for a brake job, I expect that they are competent and will fix my brakes.

I have met planners and advisors whose business cards have lots of letters after their names. The fact that they have these certifications and credentials does not guarantee nor is it a predictor of a practice with growing revenues.

Joe Polish is a highly accomplished marketer and founder of *The Genius Network*. He is also a student of Dan Kennedy and Gary Halbert. In his own words, as stated on his website (GeniusNetwork.com), "Genius Network is the exclusive group where high-level entrepreneurs meet to get their next BIG breakthrough. Gain access to connection, contribution, and collaboration, not available anywhere else."

When I asked Polish what his definition of marketing was, he responded, *"Marketing is what you do to get potential clients on the phone or in your office properly positioned so that they are pre-interested, pre-motivated, pre-qualified, and predisposed to do business with you."*

Not to be a jerk, but please explain to me how an acronym on your business card **that your prospects don't understand** meets Joe's test. It doesn't. Folks outside the financial services industry don't know what CFA®, CRPC®, CRPS®, and RICP® are. Why would they?

Running a successful and growing practice is not about credentials. It is about attracting the right prospects and convincing them to do business with you. Having credentials definitely helps, but it is not a prerequisite for success in our business.

Unfortunately, I have met many advisors and planners who have a *marketing reluctance,* fueled by the belief that because they hold a CFA® or CFP® designation, they should not be <u>required</u> to market their practice and they are above that sort of thing. Nothing could be further from the truth.

7. MARKETING IS ONE AND DONE, NOT A SEQUENCE OF STEPS.

Dan Kennedy taught me that if I am marketing to a group of prospects and I only send one message, I might as well not do anything at all. 'Nuff said.

8. MARKETING FUNNELS ARE OUTDATED; EVERYONE CAN'T BE MARKETED THE SAME WAY.

Someone explained marketing to me at a marketing conference in Cleveland. Think of a funnel. When you meet someone who may be a prospect, when you get a referral who is a potential client, *drop* them into the top of the funnel and market them all the same way. Perhaps it is this kind of a sequence:

- A handwritten card along with a copy of your special report
- An e-mail
- An autographed copy of your book
- A letter
- Another e-mail
- An invitation to lunch
- Another handwritten card

You get the idea. The important thing is, there are no *one-offs*. Everyone is dropped into the funnel and marketed in an identical manner. **Yes, you will tweak your message for the engineer versus the retail store owner, but remember, it's** a system—**a marketing system**. Think McDonald's. Every hamburger in every town in every state in America is made the same way. There are no rogue hamburger makers. McDonald's has a system, and it is followed to the letter. That is how a world-class marketing system works.

9. BASIC MARKETING CONCEPTS ARE A THING OF THE PAST.

There is a well known marketing formula that goes like this: problem, agitate, solve. Simply put, state the problem to the prospect, agitate the problem in the prospect's mind and invalidate all other solutions other than your own, and solve the problem for the prospect. It might seem simple, but this formula is responsible for billions in sales.

Another well known formula is AIDA, which stands for *Attention, Interest, Desire, and Action*. According to Wikipedia, it is an acronym for a model that is "widely used in marketing and advertising to describe the steps or stages that occur from the time when a consumer first becomes aware of a product or brand through to when the consumer trials a product or makes a purchase decision."

Personally, I have never read a financial services firm marketing department brochure that effectively uses either of these time-tested techniques.

But what about you? You can certainly implement them. Let's see what's keeping you from doing that.

5

Four Obstacles to Marketing

. . . .

The Ones That Are Extremely Difficult to Overcome

Good writing is invisible to the reader—he should not be aware he's reading something. Instead, your copy should smoothingly melt into the conversation already going on in his head.

—John Carlton

We're going to look now at what keeps financial advisors from marketing—obstacles they either ignore or view as insurmountable.

1. FAS AND MARKETING INCEST

Think back to grade school. There were always kids who cheated off the kid at the next desk. Whether that kid was smart or dumb mattered little. The point was that the cheater could obtain the desired result—finishing the exam—with little effort.

Fast forward 25 years, and we see advisors copying what other advisors are doing. This is no better than cheating off the dumb kid at the next desk. Could we go so far as to call it marketing incest?

Many advisors find themselves imitating the advisor who doesn't know what he or she is doing. Crappy results are multiplied because no one is thinking strategically.

2. FAS OFTEN HAVE NO MARKETING ROLE MODELS

Financial advisors' offices are seldom staffed with individuals who are great or even somewhat good marketers. There is no one to ask, no one to bounce ideas off of, no one to collaborate with—in effect, there are no marketing role models.

The staff at the home office has their own challenges, and baby-sitting you and your marketing problems is probably not high on their list.

3. FAS OFTEN ARE NOT WILLING TO SPEND MONEY ON MARKETING

While it is embarrassing to admit, most advisors I have spoken to are very cheap when it comes to ponying up marketing dollars. They have no problem springing for lunches or dinners, but investing in a marketing project or, better yet, a system is something many are unwilling to do.

I am convinced that financial advisors have no idea how effective a finely tuned, multi-layered marketing system can be.

4. FAS ARE UNAWARE OF THE POWER OF DIRECT RESPONSE MARKETING

Seldom have I seen an effective marketing system at work in our business. I have seen systems work with dry cleaners, tax prep firms, carpet cleaners, and dentists.

While I have faith that there are some planners and advisors out there who are using direct response marketing and effectively implementing marketing funnels, a whole lot more needs to take place.

MARKET THE WHO, NOT THE THING

Let me tell you a story...

Financial advisors are **everywhere**. But there's one advisor in practically every town in America who fits the following description. Their face, message, and contact information can be found in the local paper, sponsoring the kids' summer camp, active in the local Chamber, displayed on the back of buses and at bus stops. They host a local financial radio show on Saturday mornings, teach a class at the community college, and sponsor the Women's League *Night on the Town.*

They have written special reports and books that they give away. They mail monthly newsletters to all their clients, to CPAs, to attorneys, to store owners. They have direct mail campaigns that run all year long. They have unique websites that act as a funnel for prospects to be drawn into their marketing machines. They are ubiquitous. Everywhere you turn, you see their ads and messages. Other advisors typically hate this person, but the intelligent course of action is to dissect and understand all their marketing strategies.

What is worth noting is that these hypothetical advisors most likely are not marketing a **product**. These advisors are marketing **themselves**.

If you are competing with this person in your town, you won't stand a chance unless you can differentiate yourself in some important ways and connect with prospects on an emotional level. Keeping reality at arm's length will do you no good. There's an old movie line that says you don't bring a knife to gunfights.

Find a way to market to your prospects. You need to market values such as financial security for their family, college education for their kids without overwhelming debt, and an independent retirement for themselves. Help them make proper decisions about Social Security, long-term care insurance, and retirement plans. What's important is that you find a way to establish an *emotional connection*. That's often accomplished with repetition. Never do any marketing just once. The watchword here is that everything you do should be part of a sequence.

You may choose to market or not. So which is it? The health of your practice hangs in the balance. It depends on how you answer that question. You obviously don't want to market your services *or yourself* as a repetitive experience. You don't want it to be routine like getting a cavity drilled every year or mandatory fasting for blood tests at the doctor's office. So how do you veer away from the routine and offer an exceptional experience and menu of services?

Often the answer is to look outside our industry. Search for interesting marketing ideas at local businesses that have nothing to do with our industry. Watch what the local manufacturing company, realtors, and dentists are doing with their marketing.

Don't fall into the trap of thinking your business is different. It's not.

Look through the offers you receive in Val-Pack and other direct mail campaigns. There's a lot of commerce going on out there, and you can be sure you don't hold all the great ideas in your head. You never know where your next great idea will come from. You can gain a lot of ideas if you simply look for them. Keep in mind that the question you must ask yourself is this: *How can I **apply this** to my business?*

Whatever marketing strategies you eventually decide to implement, remember that they must be managed. Marketing is not something you set and forget. There may be necessary complexities even in a simple four-step *client acquisition* or *lead generation marketing* campaign. And here's the most important thing: Market ***yourself***, not your product.

How Firms
View Financial
Advisor Marketing

. . . .

Say Hello to Your Corporate
Marketing Department

The right message scribbled on scratch paper in crayon –
delivered to the right prospect – will outsell fancy brochures
designed by award winning graphic artists – every time.

—**Russell J. Martino,** Master Direct Response Copywriter

IMAGINE ENLISTING IN THE MARINES and being sent to Parris Island, South Carolina, for basic training. You get off the bus with dozens of other recruits and scan the 8,000-plus-acre landscape that will be your home for the next 13 weeks. Here, you will leave your civilian life behind and adopt a military mindset. Yet the first thing on your mind as you hop off the bus is that you're famished and can't wait to eat.

You walk up to the nearest officer and ask directions to the nearest restaurant that serves a rib-eye steak and mashed potatoes. The officer looks at you like you're crazy and proceeds to inform you that you will eat nothing but gruel and toast for the next 13 weeks. He further explains that the Marines would be hard pressed to offer individualized *dining experiences* due to a lack of chefs and not giving a damn. He kicks your butt back into line as you suddenly realize that your choices are severely limited.

Welcome to your corporate marketing department!

MY ANTI-CORPORATE-BROCHURE BIAS

If you would like a variety of marketing tools to help grow your practice, get used to the idea that those tools will have to come from *you*—not the corporate marketing department. Likewise, if you want a rib eye steak at Parris Island, your momma best cook you one and mail it to you in a care package. Whether it ever reaches you in your bunk is another story. And you can forget the mashed potatoes; they don't travel well.

Don't get me wrong, I don't hate corporate marketing departments. I just feel that the materials they generally provide are of limited value in landing me a new client. So yes, I guess I do have a **corporate anti-brochure bias**. Let me explain.

Glossy Wall Street type brochures with pretty pictures of active seniors holding their grandchildren make marketing departments proud. Their associates huddle around large conference tables debating background colors, stock photos, page count, and copy design.

All the while, they're being very careful about the words they use, not wanting the compliance department to tell them, "*You can't say that!*" Yet I look at their products, and they have **nothing** to do with the nitty gritty, meticulous, number-crunching, hours-long, detail-oriented planning that goes into delivering the <u>outstanding</u> work you and I do for our clients. Clients have no clue of the hours that planners and advisors spend comparing solutions in order to come up with the best choices to implement.

Marketing department pamphlets fall far short in this area. And the language they use is so *corporate*—a sanitized form of communication that people do not use when they speak to each other.

Here is an example of a corporate brochure and why I am biased against them:

> *As your Financial Advisor, I can help you define and strive to meet your goals by delivering a vast array of resources to you in the way that is most appropriate for how you invest and what you want to achieve. Working together, I can help you to preserve and grow your wealth. You will have access to some of the world's most seasoned and respected investment professionals, a premier trading and execution platform, and a full spectrum of investment choices.*

I seriously doubt that the above sentences inserted into a three-panel pamphlet—you know the one with background, education, certifications, and five choices of background scenes—has ever convinced anyone to do business with you.

Imagine the following conversation going on in your prospect's home at 8:00 in the evening: *Ya know, honey, that three-panel brochure from that advisor we met with really speaks to me. Did you know that two brothers founded that firm in 1972 in Duluth, Minnesota?*

It seems as if the marketing departments of many firms go out of their way to depersonalize their marketing materials. It's as if they want prospects to form a bond with the firm rather than the planner or advisor. That speaks to the decades-long battle in the financial services community of who the client *actually belongs to*—the advisor or the firm.

Many of the old guard wire houses insist that the client belongs to the firm. Others have taken the position that clients are served by the advisor, and the firm is there to just back up the advisor and provide a menu of services to support them. Regardless of who is right, most marketing pieces are impersonal, typically large, expensive periodicals.

WHAT ARE THOSE FAUX GENERAL INTEREST MAGAZINES?

One of the newer offerings touted by financial services marketing departments is the *faux general interest magazine*. They are professionally designed glossy magazines printed quarterly. Firms are quick to say "They are designed to complement your business with topics that can be used as starting points for important conversations with clients".

Generally, an advisor is given one or two pages of the 60-page magazine for personal dialogue with clients and prospects. The message generally begins something like this:

I hope you enjoy this issue of New Jersey Today, featuring an in-

terview with John Smith who lost everything, but through care-
ful financial planning was able to claw his way back and build a
powerful company that today provides New Jerseyites with clean
drinking water! Also tucked within the pages of this issue you'll
discover the grandeur and wonder of the Grand Canyon. If you
haven't made an appointment to update your financial plan,
please call Bobby in our office at (201) 555-1212 for an appoint-
ment today!

These magazines feature a variety of articles, sometimes including the following:

◆ Summertime – time to head to the beach!
◆ A twist on the humble peach cobbler
◆ Estate planning – a family affair
◆ Touring downtown Charleston in the fall
◆ Last-minute travel trips

While we can all agree that stories about beach travel, peach cobbler, and travel tips are entertaining, how do they advance the relationship and trust factor with a financial advisor? The answer is ***they don't***. Magazines like these serve a purpose for the advisor's firm but do nothing to enhance the advisor's image in the eyes of his or her clients.

I think the faux magazine fails the marketing smell test on several fronts. First, if an advisor simply wants to keep his or her name in front of clients, there are easier and cheaper ways to do that.

Goodyear has no illusions that by parking a blimp over a football game you will run out at half time and buy a new pair of snow tires. If that were its goal, the company could have saved a boatload of money by not building a blimp, buying the helium, renting a hangar, and hiring a pilot.

Second, any financial advisor marketing tool should attempt to *enter the conversations already going on in their prospects' minds*, such as saving for the triple financial threats of retirement, their children's education, and weddings. These three ideas pack a lot more punch than peach cobbler and Charleston in the fall. They speak directly to the ongoing worries or concerns their prospects may be experiencing.

FA MARKETING—INDIVIDUALIZED OR CORPORATE?

I can easily detect brochures that bear the *marketing department look*—slick, stock pictures and impersonal, very high-end quality. They generally include vague and happy language about how we work with you, our history, our commitment to excellence, and so on. I think of it as the **myth** of individualized FA marketing—brought to you by your marketing department.

I'm sure the marketing associates work very hard at what they do, but experience has shown me that their products are often of limited value. If you will allow me a short rant, I'll ask the following questions:

- ♦ Who staffs these departments?
- ♦ Is it their first job out of college?
- ♦ Have they ever sold anything nose-to-nose, toes-to-toes?
- ♦ Do they have real-world selling and marketing experience?
- ♦ Have they ever studied Gary Halbert, Dan Kennedy, John Carlton, Gary Bencivenga, Jay Abraham, or Chet Holmes?

◆ Are they sent to marketing conferences to learn from master marketers *outside their industry?*

MY ANTI-CORPORATE-POWERPOINT-PRESENTATION BIAS

I also have a **corporate anti-PowerPoint presentation bias**. Let me explain.

I have reviewed countless PowerPoint presentations made available by marketing departments that allow planners and advisors to literally *fill in the blanks*. Page after page is vague and general copy about planning processes, research, and accountability.

The presentations violate the prime rule of <u>no more than three points per page</u>. Often, these presentations are copy-dense with three to four paragraphs of small print filling up 18 pages. An additional six pages are reserved for a myriad of disclaimers that are seldom read by anyone yet mandated by the compliance folks, the SEC, or FINRA.

Make no mistake, if your PowerPoint presentation includes print that is too small for the entire room to read, you have just proved you have poor judgment. And if you say something like *I know this is too small to read, but...,* someone in the room will be muttering under their breath about the imbecile in the front of the room. Don't let that happen to you!

YOUR OWN MARKETING MATERIAL— HOW IS IT POSSIBLE?

Because of the limitations imposed by your firm and regulators, you might think you shouldn't even try to create your own marketing material. But you would be wrong. Experience has shown me that I can create *copy* that passes compliance inspection with little difficulty. In fact, I have written hundreds of compliance-department-approved pieces.

First and foremost, you must abide by the prohibition against testimonials of any kind. But don't let that throw you; there is plenty to say that doesn't include testimonials from satisfied clients who think you walk on water. Also, stay away from performance claims of all kinds. Forget about telling folks how your strategies lower risk and increase returns. You can say plenty about your practice without straying into grey territory and being shot down by the compliance department over unsubstantiated claims.

A number of interesting marketing ideas have come from asset management organizations that work with financial planners, broker dealers, and independent RIAs. In fact, many have provided advisors with templates of *bring-a-friend activities* that may be used to attract prospects. Consider hiring a photographer to memorialize the event. You will want to send framed pictures to participants along with a hand written note. Here are some examples:

- Advisor hosts a cooking class with a professional chef to teach clients and their friends how to prepare a world-class meal; then everyone dines together.
- Advisor hosts a coffee-tasting class with a professional coffee roaster.
- Advisor hosts a lunch with a local golf pro at a country club, and everyone gets putting lessons after lunch.
- Advisor hosts a craft beer or wine-tasting event.

You might decide to write your own brochures or special reports that highlight your unique processes. They might include your own signature story, pitfalls to avoid, or behavior that enhances wealth. You could also write some detailed case studies and compare successful planning to someone who tries to *wing it*.

The choices are limitless. But above all, use your imagination and make it fit you and your practice.

7

Own Your Own Media

· · · · · · ·

Have You Ever Thought about That?

If you can arrange it, be born into money; preferably a vast fortune. Failing that be born with world-class good looks, with a heaping helping of acting, musical, or athletic talent. If you are unable to arrange for these things and still seek unlimited wealth and freedom, become a direct response copywriter. It will afford you wealth and freedom that is otherwise reserved for the world's most fortunate elite.

—Clayton Makepeace

THERE'S A NEVER-ENDING array of ideas to choose from when it comes to marketing. And even if you don't fancy yourself a Ted Turner, you might consider owning your own media. **No,** I haven't gone off the deep end and suggested that you buy a radio station or big city newspaper. I'm talking about having *multiple media platforms.* Here are some thoughts for you to consider:

- Send out a monthly, printed, mailed newsletter directed to your clients, prospects, and centers of influence. There are services that provide these types of mailings inexpensively and, most importantly, work with your compliance department so all articles are approved. You can write a feature article each month that will appear on page 1.

- Suppose for a moment that you surveyed your book of business and discovered that six plumbers have accounts with you. Let us further suppose that you contact them and arrange to speak at the next Northeast Plumbing Alliance meeting. Maybe you could also figure out a way to appear as a guest columnist focusing on retirement issues in their monthly newsletter that goes out to all 230 members who own plumbing companies.

- What about writing a (compliance-approved) weekly blog and posting it on LinkedIn or other social media? Consider choosing a complex theme (for example, common mistakes when choosing beneficiaries) that can be broken down into a number of posts over a period of time.

- Ever thought about having your own podcast or radio show? Sure, it's not simple, but they can provide broad exposure over a long period of time. There are many services that will help you explore whether this alternative is appropriate and cost-effective for you.

- Why not write a book? I'm not asking you to be Ernest Hemmingway or Louisa May Alcott. The objective of writing a book is not to land you on the *New York Times* Best Seller list. The book should be designed as a *lead generation magnet* that can be used as the foundation for all future marketing. No longer will you press your card into a prospect's hand; you will give them a signed copy of your book.

These are just five examples of media platforms. There are many others you may want to consider. What they all have in common is that they are a form of media where you can spread the message of who you are, why you do what you do, and why you are different than the competition.

Media platforms give you the opportunity to ***make your message personal and compelling***. And that's something your marketing department most likely will not do.

8

What I Learned from Other Professions

· · · · · · ·

Some Essentials to Understand

*I don't know one way to get 15 new clients a year, but
I know 15 ways to get one new client a year.*

—Unknown

THE TIME SPENT creating and refining a marketing strategy can be some of the most valuable time you spend in your career. Growth does not happen by accident, and seldom does it happen in the absence of intelligent planning.

EXPECT REVENUE GROWTH

An advisor should have no expectations of revenue growth in the absence of a carefully thought out marketing strategy.

Best-selling author Mark Victor Hansen tells the story of approaching a loan officer at a bank early in his career, well before *Chicken Soup for the Soul* fame. When he asked about the process of applying for a loan, the banker replied that he would need a statement, referring to a statement of assets and liabilities. Hansen, still rather young, did not have money or a balance sheet. So when he was asked for a statement, he replied, "I'm optimistic!" The banker was not amused at the young man's flippant reply.

Are you optimistic about revenue growth for your practice? If you don't have a solid, well thought out marketing plan, you have *no reason* to be optimistic. That's no different from driving from Phoenix to the Bronx with a vague notion that you must go east.

CREATE A LOT OF OPEN DOORS

As you begin to piece together a marketing strategy, understand that there may be a variety of components that work together. Remember, advisors don't need great results from one idea; they need okay results from a lot of marketing ideas. In effect, **you are creating a lot of open doors for prospective clients to walk through.**

Here is an example of many *open doors* created by one advisor who gives away great information to prospects and clients:

- Wrote special reports on important retirement subjects
- Engineered a method for radio stations to call for interviews
- Wrote a book about financial challenges in retirement
- Writes articles for real estate agent newsletters
- Posts blogs to LinkedIn
- Contacts local service organizations to speak at meetings
- Writes a monthly newsletter for COIs, prospects, and clients

♦ Appears as a guest columnist in two industry newsletters

In 2019, I sat in a Dallas hotel conference room listening to billionaire wealth manager Ken Fisher, the owner of Fisher Investments; describe how he grew his firm from virtually nothing to $97 billion of assets under management. He emphasized that ***direct response marketing*** was the cornerstone of his marketing strategy.

Additionally, he spoke of using *all* of the following methods that have placed Fisher Investments in the minds of qualified prospects:

♦ Write investment column for *Forbes* magazine
♦ Use direct mail
♦ Write investment books
♦ Place ads on the radio
♦ Advertise on TV
♦ Purchase magazine ads
♦ Purchase newspaper ads
♦ Use Internet ads

DEVELOP A MESSAGE-TO-MARKET MATCH

Targeting is a concept lost on many financial advisors. You need to be certain you are directing your message to an audience that is receptive to hearing it and has the ability and desire to act. Here are two examples that illustrate this from my broker dealer days.

First, consider the advisor who decides, <u>without any preparation or research</u>, to blanket mail a 529 college savings message to an apartment complex full of 20 something singles. The message wasn't crafted for them. **Wrong message—wrong audience.** This is a classic example of ready, fire, aim.

Even worse is the advisor who held a seminar in the common room at a retirement community for 20 senior citizens with a pitch about small-cap investing. The advisor was viewed as a product pusher, hawking a totally inappropriate product for an older, conservative audience. Again, the **wrong product presented to the wrong audience**. There was **no message-to-market match**. The result was a frustrated and embarrassed advisor who wasted a lot of time and money for no results.

Message-to-market match is a critical component of the marketing strategy—in any line of business. Consider the carpet cleaner who mails an offer to all homes in the zip code east of his business, only to find out that they are the worst looking rental homes with neglected lawns, rusted cars up on blocks in the driveways, and absolutely **no interest** in cleaning their carpets.

Had the carpet cleaner done some research, had he just taken the time to drive by in his truck street by street, he would have bypassed that area of town in favor of nicer homes with well kept lawns whose owners may have an interest in a professional coming to clean and sanitize their carpets.

DO ONE THING EACH DAY TO MARKET YOUR BUSINESS

There are tens of thousands of people within 50 miles of your office who may be a suitable client of your practice. The problem is, they have never heard of you. How you choose to solve the problem is something you need to spend some quality time thinking about.

Several enterprising advisors I know make it a habit to gift their special reports to all owners and managers of businesses they frequent. One goes as far as gifting his reports to the pilots on every airplane he rides on.

One of my favorite ways to market is to be a *resource* to prospects and clients and be a valuable connector to others whose services they are looking for. I become a virtual million-dollar Rolodex®. You can accomplish that by networking and by being a go-giver. Always look to give before you get. Be known as the person who <u>always offers to help</u>, and you will be surprised at how many people will be drawn to you.

CULTIVATE LIFETIME CLIENT VALUE

Lifetime client value is an often misunderstood or unknown concept. Assuming you run a fee-based advisory practice, let's consider a straightforward example:

A $2,000,000 client acquired with $200,000 held in cash and CDs and $1.8 million under management at a fee of 1.1% **plus** a $12,500 financial planning fee:

$ 12,500   planning fee
<u>$121,907</u>   Fee for years 1 through 5 assuming 5% annual growth
$134,407   Total 5-year revenues (numbers are approximate)

Many financial advisors have never looked at their marketing from this perspective. Given the numbers above, <u>would it be unreasonable</u> to suggest that an advisor might spend $100, $500, or $1,000 *or more* to gain such a client?

What about $3,000 or even $5,000? Most professionals would default to the widespread answer that they would like to spend *the least amount of money* to bring in a new client. With that mindset, would you like to compete against an advisor who is willing to spend thousands to gain a new client?

After all, the advisor who is willing to spend more may have additional marketing tools at his or her disposal to attract the multi-million-dollar client. For example, that advisor might provide the prospect with a personalized *shock and awe package* prior to the first meeting, delivered by FedEx, which virtually guarantees the prospect will open the package. The package might contain special reports, a personal letter, or books written by the advisor, along with interesting and appropriately priced gifts such as a fireproof document bag or a leather-bound statement binder.

What if the prospect receives this the same week as *your* envelope containing the marketing department's special three-panel color pamphlet, complete with your name and bio?

Do you see where I am going with this? Personally, I am willing to outspend my competition in order to *outmarket them* with the goal of securing the multi-million-dollar prospect, converting them to a fee-paying client and expanding my practice.

So I ask you again. How much would you be willing to spend to gain a new client with similar or larger numbers?

ESTABLISH A USP (UNIQUE SELLING PROPOSITION)

Another thing I learned from other professions and from other professionals is to establish a USP (unique selling proposition). You might simply call it your focus. What is the main focal point of your business? Who are you targeting? What specific service are you providing?

Here are some examples of a USP from my team:

♦ **We maximize retirement clarity**—we help create and execute effective, efficient, and comprehensive retirement strategies for the business owner clients we serve.
♦ **We advise and collaborate** in the **design** and **implementation** of customized retirement accumulation and income strategies for entrepreneurs.
♦ Our team provides the expertise and resources needed to **manage the complexities of significant wealth.**
♦ **We work with entrepreneurial family leaders 50 and older** who have achieved financial success and need our experience and expertise to create retirement income strategies that preserve their wealth and maintain their desired standard of living.

Now what does your business look like? Take some time to write it down.

♦ What are the focus and objective for your business?
♦ Describe in detail the type of clients you serve best.
♦ What precise services do you provide them?
♦ Why should they have confidence in **you**?

Authority Marketing

Separating Yourself from the Competition

*My definition of marketing is simple—it's all about educating the
marketplace that your business can solve problems, fill voids, or
achieve opportunities and goals the way no other business can.*

—**Jay Abraham**

WE'VE COME A long way on this journey through the world
of financial advisors and marketing. I've given you an introductory
glimpse of marketing ideas and strategies, as well as sound advice
from Dan Kennedy.

Now I want to share with you how <u>making marketing a study</u> has
changed my life. Prior to 2013, I had never heard the term *direct
response marketing*. But in addition to learning the fundamentals of
direct response marketing, newsletters, and direct mail strategies, I
also learned about **authority marketing.**

MAKE YOURSELF AN AUTHORITY

Prior to discovering Dan Kennedy, the amount of time I spent on marketing was essentially zero. Make no mistake, I worked 60 to 65 hours a week and was busy all day, but I was working *in* my business and not *on* my business. As a result of what I learned, I accomplished the following *marketing wins*:

- Wrote my first book, ***Forging Bonds of Steel: How to Build a Successful and Lasting Relationship with Your Financial Advisor,*** in 2014. It added more than a dozen names to my client list, millions in assets under management, and more financial planning fees.
- Released my second book, ***Fire Your Retirement Planner: YOU! Concise Advice on How to Join the $100,000 Retirement Club***, in 2016. This compilation of 52 blog posts, categorized by subject, added clients, increased assets under management, and multiplied financial plans.
- Published my third book, ***The Mindset of Retirement Success: 7 Winning Strategies to Change Your Life***, in 2017. Laid out a strategy that made me *magnetic* to radio talk show hosts, and then I appeared on radio more than 35 times. And yes, I got more clients and more assets.
- Wrote my fourth book, ***Parent's Guide to Your Child's Retirement: 21 Thought Provoking Conversations to Have with Your Adult Child***, in 2018. It was a home run! It cemented client relationships and strengthened their view of me as *their sole trusted family advisor*.
- Wrote more than 150 articles and blogs and a dozen special reports.
- Sponsored *Evening with the Author* presentations.
- Presented my books at various service organizations.

HOW IT CHANGED ME

My daily routine was altered dramatically. I now carry five to seven special reports with me wherever I go. I give them to:

1. Gas station owners
2. Auto repair shops
3. Managers at the grocery store
4. Accountants and attorneys
5. Real estate agents
6. Owners of the local gym
7. Restaurant owners
8. People wherever I shop
9. Airline pilots
10. Franchise owners
11. Truckers

I have given away hundreds of these inexpensive special reports. Why would I give out a business card when these special reports at the cost of about a dollar have so much more impact? My reports are on display in my dentist's office and in my doctor's office. They create a buzz about my practice. My special reports speak directly to my target market, and I am entering the conversation they are already having in their minds about their future financial security and independence. They have a million unanswered questions about retirement, and I position myself as a knowledgeable resource.

In addition to my special reports, I have created a 16-page *special edition* newsletter chocked full of timeless articles, quizzes, and information on our team. It is designed to capture the eyes and attention of those who are serious about preparing for retirement. The newsletter includes special offers for my books and special reports, as well as free information. It introduces people to me—*The Professor of Harsh Retirement Reality*—and my persona as an author and an expert. It gives them confidence in my **expertise**.

I am happy to give away hundreds of these newsletters rather than business cards. The black and white newsletter is deliberately ugly and plain, designed for easy reading. One look at it and you know it did not come from a corporate marketing department.

I am giving folks a taste of what it's like to have *me and my team* in their world. The provocative questions I ask and the ideas I present take them out of their comfort zone and give them a glimpse of what it would be like to work with my financial planning team.

All of these marketing strategies are ongoing activities, and I am passionate about getting them out there 24/7. And here is the interesting part: it's not even work; it's fun.

WHAT I'VE LEARNED, WHO I SHARE IT WITH

This is just *some of what I learned* and executed as a result of understanding that **marketing is the primary function of my business.** Oh, and in case you were wondering, writing a book is not all that difficult. Remember, the purpose of the book is to be a *lead generation magnet*, not to land you on the *New York Times* Best Seller list. I engage in all these activities to create numerous doors for prospects to walk through and learn more about me and my team.

I have spent six years immersing myself in marketing. I've read scores of books and explored Dan Kennedy, Jay Abraham, Gary

Halbert, John Carlton, Brian Tracy, and others. The marketing strategies and tactics I have *learned and implemented* are responsible for huge increases in my revenues. The results have been life-changing.

I am now taking everything I have learned and much of what I have written and making it available to select financial advisors who agree that the marketing of their practice is vitally important in personal wealth building.

The Architecture of Authority

· · · · · · ·

Who Knows More about You Than You?

Tactics without strategy is the noise before defeat.

—SunTzu, *The Art of War*

SCAN THE PROMOTION and advertising pieces available to you through your firm's marketing department, and you will most likely come to the same conclusion I did. There is *nothing* in their catalogue of materials that will showcase your practice in any compelling way.

In fact, most, if not all, marketing materials are plain vanilla, written by newly minted marketing graduates and then sanitized by your compliance department. The resulting product is boring, uninteresting, and bland. There is a sameness to it.

The reason it looks like it was created by a corporate advertising department is because a corporate advertising department created it. If you think the three-panel brochure looks like every other advisor's three-panel brochure, **you are right**. They are all boilerplate, except for your bio. Oh, and you can choose from six landscapes and three color themes.

ENHANCING YOUR AUTHORITY

These marketing pieces will most likely do **nothing** to enhance your **authority** or favorably establish you in the minds of your prospects. In my experience, they *do not work well* as:

- A leave-behind
- A direct mail piece
- Part of an information package on your practice

In fact, I believe they are useless and should be ignored. So the question becomes this: **How do you establish authority in a meaningful way?** Think back to freshman English or 12th grade composition where you were required to write essays about things you cared nothing about. Odds are you hated the assignments and dreaded receiving a subpar grade. At least, that's what I remember. But times have changed. Now we are going to talk about writing about something that you *deeply care about*—**your practice**.

Answer these questions:

- Who knows more about your practice than you?
- Who could best articulate what you do for your clients?
- Who cares most about how your practice is viewed?
- Who is most passionate about your practice?

◆ Who <u>worries</u> most about the outcomes your client's experience?

If I'm any judge of character, your firm's marketing department is NOT one of your answers to the above questions. So you are beginning to see and understand that if you are to promote and market your practice effectively, **you need to be involved.**

Although establishing authority is not as simple as writing an assignment, it is a good place to begin. Do you think you might be able to **write a couple of paragraphs about your practice?** I'm not asking for Pulitzer Prize–winning prose like Sinclair Lewis or Robert Penn Warren. I'm just asking for <u>a couple hundred words that describe in a compelling way what you do.</u>

Pretend you are sitting across from the perfect prospect, one that meets your client profile to a T. What would you say? Don't worry about grammar, punctuation, or rules. Just write from your heart.

Or pretend that your mom asked you to write a letter to her oldest best friend who just inherited $6 million and asked your mom for advice. Try writing a couple of drafts about the process you take your clients through, from discovery to liquidity and income needs, investment policy, risk assessment, asset allocation, and more.

Don't worry about polishing or presenting it. At this point, you just want to gauge if you can <u>intelligently define and explain what it is you do for your clients.</u> Try this multiple times, and definitely use a thesaurus. Try to use interesting words. You don't want to be bland. Leave that to your firm's marketing department!

We are talking here about <u>taking baby steps</u>. I'm not asking you to write a book, although we **can** explore and weigh **that** possibility.

Remember, as you write, no testimonials of any kind, and ditto for talking about performance. Remember, FINRA and the SEC are looking over your shoulder. Everything you write will be absolutely truthful, but **it need not be boring**. You will find buckets to write about that don't include beating the S&P.

At a later time, you can have your prose cleaned up and submitted for review to your compliance department. It's very likely that they may ask you to change a couple of items and recommend that you add a couple of disclaimers to protect you and your firm. But you may be surprised that you have come up with an approved marketing piece that showcases your practice in an <u>intelligent and compelling fashion.</u> You now have a piece of *approved copy* and there's a lot you can do with it.

What I have shown you is one building block to creating **authority**. Although the architecture of authority is complex, it all starts with one action.

As you are thinking this through, ask yourself this question:

How many of your competitors are willing
to take this kind of action?

WHO IS YOUR BEST PROSPECT, AND WHAT DO YOU DO FOR THEM?

We've talked a lot about establishing **who you are** and creating an **architecture of authority**. Now let's think about and identify **who you are for**. In order to attract your ideal prospect, <u>you must write to them</u>, to their fears, their dreams, and their desires.

Here are two valuable exercises for you. First, <u>make a list of the</u>

<u>attributes of your best prospects</u>. Who are they? Are they married, business owners, conservative, liberal, parents, government workers? Think of every adjective that describes them. At this point, you are brainstorming. Don't edit your answers; just keep making your list. The time for editing will come soon enough.

For example, you may determine that your best prospects share these attributes:

- Ages 45–55
- Married with children
- Homeowner
- Corporate executive
- Minimum annual income of $180,000
- Minimum net worth of $800,000
- Worried about retirement
- Politically conservative
- Concerned about going into debt to finance college education

The more you can narrow down *who you are for* and *who you are not for*, the better.

Here are some examples of <u>who you are not for</u>:

- Under 40 years old
- Government worker
- Single
- Believes personal finance is a do-it-yourself project
- No kids
- Annual income under $60,000
- Net worth under $200,000

KEEP NICHING DOWN

You want to keep *niching* down. After all, you can't be for everyone. You must be for a select few who are perfect matches for your practice. So keeping adding attributes. Do they read *Home and Garden* or *Business Week*? Do they bowl or play tennis? Do they belong to country clubs, or do they attend baseball games?

When you have a good-sized list, start consolidating and making sense of it. Segregate the most important features from the least important. Come up with a dozen or so primary characteristics of the profile of the client you serve best. Once you have nailed this down, the list will serve as a **filter** through which you run all prospects. And once you have carefully identified the **prime characteristics of your best clients**, you can then search only for them.

Next, make a list of everything you do well, all the services you offer, and what you **excel** at. Try to think of every reason someone would hire you.

Here are some sample areas you may excel at:

- Retirement income plans
- Financial budgeting
- Asset allocation
- IRA rollovers
- College education funding
- Retirement accumulation plans
- 401(k) specialist
- Tax-efficient investing

If you're good at it and enjoy doing it for your clients, include it on the list. Remember, you will edit your list later. The objective here is to be able to match your skills and abilities to the needs, wants, and desires of your perfect prospect.

Once you have narrowed down both of your lists to workable documents, you will have accomplished the following:

⬥ Identified **who you are**
⬥ Identified **who you are *not* for**
⬥ Identified **what you can do** for **who you are for**

If you stopped right there, you would be far ahead of most financial advisors who cannot articulate what they do or who they do it for. Most advisors opt for simple solutions. Adding great clients to your practice is not simple; it is a complex undertaking.

Remember, you will never solve a complex problem with simple solutions.

With this in mind, begin writing about the challenges your target market faces. Then begin sharing it with prospects and centers of influence, with CPAs and attorneys you know. Why not include a one- or two-page article as a free-standing insert in a monthly newsletter, or post it on *Facebook* or *LinkedIn*?

What would stop you from writing one article per week? Your goal is to connect with potential prospects and **enter the conversations already occurring in their heads**. After all, the more you know and understand them, the easier it will be to write about it.

ENTER THE CONVERSATION ALREADY GOING ON IN YOUR CLIENT'S HEAD

I've already asked you to take a stab at writing a couple hundred words that define your process and help prospects understand what you do—**your value proposition**, if you will.

That exercise may be accurately viewed as a building block. Or you might see it as using training wheels on a bike and trying like heck not to fall down. It's okay. We are in training, and NOW is the time to make mistakes. I want you to keep trying to develop a basic style that contains your personality and speaks in a true voice. Remember, this is not your firm's corporate marketing department speaking. It's **you**. I am looking for you to adopt *personality-driven marketing*, **not corporate-driven marketing**.

I have been doing this for about five years now, and occasionally I will come across something I wrote near the beginning of my writing journey. I am immediately able to determine that *it sounds like me*, that YES, this is something I would have written. So keep writing, and try to make what you write <u>meaningful</u> to your practice.

But here is the prime rule: you must write so you are entering the conversations already going on in your prospect's mind. I want you to pretend that you are crouched under the kitchen table listening to prospects' *dead-of-night conversations* about money worries and how they may never be able to retire after paying for two college educations and two weddings. Your prospects are affluent, they do have resources, but they are limited and must be allocated properly–they are worried because they do not know what you know.

Here are some sample ideas for articles or blogs you may want to write:

◆ Is it possible to manufacture a retirement paycheck of $10,000 per month?

- Is there retirement success after paying for two college educations?
- What are the important issues when considering an IRA rollover?
- Is long-term care something you really need to worry about?
- It's not necessary to beat the market to have a financially independent retirement.
- What is asset allocation, and why is it important to me?
- How does a ROTH 401(k) differ from a ROTH IRA account?
- Five important concepts to remember about investing your retirement dollars.
- Are we ever going to be able to retire?

I just gave you nine topics to get you started. I'm sure you can brainstorm dozens more. In fact, try making a list of topics and working on one each day for a full month. You may surprise yourself and end up with 30 articles at month's end. Remember, <u>you are not ready</u> to show the world or your prospects your creations. At this point, you are just creating a bank of copy. In English, that's a bunch of articles or blog posts that showcase your knowledge, expertise, and point of view. For now, it's *your bank* not to be shared with anyone.

You may wonder how I was going to tie in a recommendation. Well, here it is. The 30 ideas you have put on paper are an exercise to prime the pump and get you ready for the next step. You see, you need a degree of confidence to take the next step and to <u>very explicitly</u> tell the world why they should raise their hand and **request an appointment with you**.

SIX CORE COMPETENCIES

You will now write down, very succinctly, **six core competencies for which you have complex and sophisticated processes**. They will be a powerful statement of fact. You will spend a lot of time on this. You will edit, rewrite, and polish it until you are happy with the outcome. You will read it aloud many times so it sounds conversational, **and**, if I woke you out of a dead sleep, you would be able to say them without hesitation.

Here is an example of one team's core competency:

> **We engineer a blueprint that encompasses your most important retirement preparation issues and assist you in moving them into the *done column*.**

Make a special effort to **write powerfully**. One of your goals is to create an emotional connection with the reader. This is not the place for bland marketing department prose. Once you have enumerated each of your core competencies, you have a perfect opportunity to expand on them and explain why they are important and how they separate you from all other advisors. In fact, you can create an entire *special report* out of this. Special reports can be very effective marketing tools when used properly.

Special note: If you absolutely positively *feel* that you are incapable of writing these articles, then you will need to outsource them. My co-author Parthiv Shah can assist you with that.

Another special note: Remember, everything will be submitted to your compliance department for review and approval prior to dissemination.

11

The Essential Element of Any Financial Advisory Practice

· · · · · · ·

Growth

If I had asked my customers what they wanted,
they would have said: a faster horse.

—Henry Ford

JAKE IS A financial advisor practicing just outside a large city on the East Coast.

He has been in business for about 12 years and is *semi-independent*. In other words, he is not an employee of a large wire house and is not an RIA. He is one of many who believe they can skimp on expenses and magically develop a 70% to 80% net payout.

If only it were that easy.

If you call Jake's office, you will generally be greeted by a voicemail message on the fifth ring. It will inform you that Jake is meeting with a client and will call you back when he is free. Somehow, somewhere, Jake got the idea that this is an acceptable business practice for his mass-affluent prospects and clientele. **He is mistaken.**

Everything in an advisory practice that can be interpreted as cheap or lacking service is a negative that must be neutralized and overcome.

In his practice, Jake has become adept at cutting corners in order to save money. He's like the fellow hopelessly in debt who becomes proficient at dining out each evening for five bucks or less.

Not surprisingly, Jake's business has not grown much over the last five years. He rarely receives a referral. Long-time clients are not quick to return his calls. Clients who attend meetings in his office are unimpressed with the décor, the utilitarian furnishings, and the utter lack of artwork. There is no personality, family pictures, or mementos. The only frames adorning the walls display his certifications.

Most clients view him as comfortable and proficient, kind of like a well-worn winter coat that will eventually be replaced when it has served its purpose.

Hopefully, this does not describe your practice.

Jake mistakenly believes that his certifications are the only marketing he needs. He's like the dentists or chiropractors who hang shingles outside their new offices, mistakenly expecting a flood of new clients to beat a path to their doors. Jake never bothered to learn the first thing about marketing. He invests neither time nor money in marketing.

So what is Jake's problem? Does he suffer from a fear of marketing? Perhaps his inaction is simply a case of monstrous procrastination or denial, believing that the letters after his name are all the marketing he will ever need. Little does Jake realize that he is in **a battle for the survival of his business**.

Were I to counsel him, I might suggest that he familiarize himself with **Joe Polish's definition of marketing:**

Marketing is what you do to get potential clients on the phone or in your office properly positioned so that they are pre-interested, pre-motivated, pre-qualified and predisposed to do business with you.

GROWTH MEANS ACTION

The success of any financial advisory practice, the essential element, is **growth**. And in order for there to be growth, there must be **action**. There must be commitment. Skating might have been an option in 11th grade English, but *not here, not now*.

Were Jake to open his eyes and take a keen look at his competition, he would see advisors spending significant amounts of time and money marketing their practices to their prospects.

We have already discussed various methods of marketing and, specifically, **authority marketing**. Were Jake to intelligently employ several of those methods, he might be surprised at the uptick in revenue for his practice.

However, I would recommend that the first investment Jake makes is hiring a well trained human being to <u>answer the phone.</u>

A FOOLPROOF METHOD OF
OPENING NEW ACCOUNTS

I am often asked this: ***What do I do to market my practice?*** Interestingly, I have come to understand that the underlying question, **the real issue** in search of an answer, is this: ***Do you know <u>one way</u> to get 12 to 15 new clients each year?***

Often I smile, remembering back when I was a rookie at E. F. Hutton, opening a dozen new accounts each month using a simple tax-free bond script. While I was able to reel in investors interested in 5–10 bonds, often there were never any repeat purchases. The reason was simple; they were yield investors. If Merrill, Paine Weber, or Dean Witter had a better-yielding bond, those investors would open accounts there. It was not uncommon for investors to have accounts with brokers all over town.

Advisors today are interested in million-dollar and multi-million-dollar relationships. Interest in 5–10 bond trades has gone the way of the telephone booth.

Many advisors are ambivalent and uncertain about marketing due to the multiplicity of approaches and potential costs of implementation. Add to that the time and effort involved, and they would much rather find the elusive *done-for-you approach*. Compounding the problem is that many financial advisors have no awareness of what effective and successful marketing is.

So the question becomes this:

What are you doing to properly position prospects so they are pre-interested, pre-motivated, pre-qualified, and predisposed to do business with you?

Colleagues from California to Arkansas will ask me what the **best way** is to open multi-million-dollar accounts. I respond that *I don't know one way to open 12 accounts, but I do know 12 ways to open one account.*

This response is <u>never met</u> with a smile. Advisors want an easy, foolproof method to open new accounts with significant assets, **and**, if truth be told, they want that method to be easy, kind of a **done-for-you.**

Listed below are some of my favorite ways to attract the attention of prospects with wealth. Remember these words: *attract the attention.* I didn't say begin a relationship, and I didn't say open an account or schedule a meeting. You need to start at the beginning, and **the beginning is to let them know you exist—attract their attention.**

NOW TAKE A LOOK AT HOW TO DO THAT.

- ♦ Network with centers of influence
- ♦ Be interviewed on a local radio show
- ♦ Write a book as a *lead generation magnet*
- ♦ Write a special report to offer to prospects
- ♦ Run an ad offering a free special report on an important planning topic
- ♦ Stay active on *Facebook* or *LinkedIn* with important information or offers

◆ Consider hosting a financial podcast and interview centers of influence

While none of these activities will ever guarantee that you will open an account with significant assets, they all can be important ways to get your name out in the community and for people (the kind of people you want as clients) to know you exist.

But the most important point is *not* that you write a book or get on the radio. *The most important point is that you decide to* **do something**—to take action, to act! You will not want to copy what I do. The very act of deciding to take action will place you far ahead of those advisors still waiting for a referral from their branch managers.

12

Five Mistakes of a Financial Advisor

. . . . . .

How Not to Market Your Practice

Life is hard. And it's harder if you're stupid.

—**John Wayne**

WHAT SEPARATES SUCCESSFUL advisors from average advisors? While we could speculate all day about the possible reasons, I prefer to focus on one very particular aspect of the equation. I think that **how** advisors *market their practices* can be a true differentiator and propel them to the highest level of the planning and advisory world.

There are many methods financial advisors can use to market their practices. Here are some of them:

- ♦ Social media
- ♦ Podcasts
- ♦ Centers of influence
- ♦ Media interviews
- ♦ **Direct response mail**
- ♦ Books
- ♦ Special reports
- ♦ Speaking

I'd like to focus on **one method** from the list: *direct response mail.* Early in my career, I took a stab at direct mail. Looking back, my efforts were pitiful. As an alternative to cold calling, I was drawn to the idea of mailing pre-printed, product-focused postcards. I told myself that *I was still prospecting*, even though I wasn't using the phone, facing rejection hour after hour, day after day. Copying names and addresses from the cross directory was better than people repeatedly hanging up on me. Mutual fund companies were more than happy to send me never-ending boxes of postcards I could mail.

I experienced limited success and told myself that direct mail does not work in my business. Little did I know how wrong I was. While I could write a whole book on this subject—and maybe I will one day—for now I will review **what I did wrong** and the **numerous mistakes** I made early on.

MY FIRST MISTAKE

The biggest mistake I made was that I did **no research** beforehand. I simply decided that mailing postcards would be a good idea. In fact, I looked around at what others (in the bull pen) were doing, and I did the same thing.

Many years later, I learned that if you don't have a great role model, you'll probably look at what everyone else is doing. **Don't do that!** The credit goes to **Earl Nightingale** for this simple but effective statement of genius. I violated his rule by believing that my success would come by copying what others were doing. Worse yet, I copied what other rookies were doing!

MY SECOND MISTAKE

My second mistake was that I didn't have an effective mailing list. Now I know that the **#1 success driver of direct mail is the *list*.** Many direct response-marketing experts believe that <u>the list</u> counts for 50% of the success of any mailing campaign.

My amateur effort had me hand-addressing postcards by streets in nice neighborhoods in my county. The street address was the only thing I knew about the people who would receive my mailing. I was setting myself up for failure, and **I was clueless.**

Little did I know that there were many types of lists. I simply scraped up names from a reverse directory, not realizing that there were also *response* lists and *compiled* lists. I wasted a tremendous amount of time—time that could have better be used by cold calling with an effective script.

I quickly came to the mistaken conclusion that direct mail doesn't work in my business!

MY THIRD MISTAKE

My best clients remained with me due to the trusting relationship we had formed over time. My third mistake was that the idea of <u>never leading with a product</u> was lost on me.

MY FOURTH MISTAKE

And then I made my fourth mistake. I violated one of the prime rules of direct marketing: Never—ever—mail just once.

Any mailing should be *part of a sequence*. For example, send a letter, and then follow it up with a postcard, a follow-up call, and then another letter. A stand-alone product postcard has almost no hope of success.

MY FIFTH MISTAKE

My mailing said this: "We have a mutual fund that does X." There was no good reason for anyone to read the entire bland message. There was nothing to draw them in and keep them reading.

I'm certain I made several more mistakes with those mailings. But you get the idea. The lessons here are numerous, but remember this:

Countless FAs are never taught how to effectively market their practices. They have been taught about financial planning, stocks, bonds, mutual funds, estate planning, retirement accounts, taxation, and more.

But they have been taught little—if anything—about marketing and growing their practices.

GET OFF YOUR BUTT AND TAKE ACTION

I have spoken with scores of financial advisors about their marketing practices, read many marketing books geared for the advisor audience, and had the opportunity to speak with industry experts such as Steve Gresham, Nick Murray, Duncan McPherson, Mitch Anthony, Russ Alan Prince, and Frank Maselli. Over decades, each of these individuals has made significant contributions to the *financial services industry's vault of knowledge* and have earned well deserved praise for their achievements. Their speeches, books, and one-on-one coaching are responsible for propelling many financial planning, wealth management, and advisory practices to high levels of success.

While they all have specific ideas on what makes a great practice and how best to grow a practice, they differ on specifics. Yet they **all agree** on this: Nothing happens until you get off your butt and take action. Whether you plan a referral campaign, a direct mail project, Medicare seminars, social media marketing, or a book, here are some of the key ingredients:

- Do research before beginning.
- Talk with others who have done what you intend to do.
- Figure out exactly what you are trying to accomplish. What is your purpose?
- Sketch out a workable plan with all necessary steps.
- Refine your plan.
- How much time, effort, and dollars will be needed to accomplish your plan?
- Define your budget.
- Will you need the help of others?
- Do you intend to involve other advisors, or is this a solo project?
- Do you need the approval of your compliance department?
- What arrangements have to be made? When? By whom?
- What is your time line?
- How will you measure success?

It's easy to see that you don't just decide that **X** might be a good idea and then go out and do it. Unfortunately, the easiest part of any project might be writing a check before everything else has been thought out. You definitely want to save <u>the money</u> <u>part</u> until you have gone through most, if not all, of the other steps.

I want to circle back to one item on the above list. It's perhaps the most important item—**What is your purpose?** You need to decide what you are really trying to accomplish. In other words, **you need clarity**. Are you looking to *get your name out there*? Are you looking to expand your list of prospects? Is your purpose to increase your authority and celebrity? Or are you trying to open new accounts and gain clients? Without a very specific idea of what your end game is, you will most likely expend a lot of energy for little or no return.

An interesting idea I learned from *marketer extraordinaire Dan Kennedy* is that we shouldn't be trailblazers. If what you are considering has never been done before, there may be a very good reason for that. Perhaps countless others have investigated and considered it and then decided it was not worth the time, effort, money, and aggravation to pursue it. Trailblazers, he says, "often end up with arrows in their backs."

What does it mean if no advisor has ever imprinted their *unique selling proposition* on a can of Spam?

13

Innovative Marketing Ideas

· · · · · · ·

The High-End Aluminum Briefcase

I know the mind, like the parachute, is most valuable open.

—**Dan Kennedy**

ONE WAY TO avoid being an unsuccessful trailblazer is to see what's working in industry A and figure out **how it can be applied** to industry B. Or, better yet, <u>how can you apply it to *your* business?</u>

WHO INVENTED IT—AND CAN YOU USE IT?

Do you think the local car dealership invented the tent sale? How about drive-through fast food, drive-through pharmacy, or same-day dry cleaning? All these *concepts* were borrowed from other industries and applied elsewhere.

What about the Tampa-based dental office with *massage chairs*, *refreshments*, and a *reading library* stocked with hundreds of books you can take home with you? Does that sound like your local dentist? I think not. This astute doctor looked at the least attractive aspects of a dental office and took it upon himself to create a stellar experience by borrowing ideas from others and using them for the benefit of his patients.

Or how about the Louisiana-based electrical component repair company that markets for new business in a very unique way. By FedEx, it sends potential customers a high-end aluminum briefcase. Inside are a DVD player, plates, forks, and a scrumptious cake to eat while watching the enclosed 18-minute video. When someone first opens the specially designed briefcase, a video plays with a personal message from Walter Bergeron, the owner of the company. He explains what's in the case and why it was sent to them. Not too many electrical repair facilities use this strategy to describe the types of equipment they fix in their facilities.

According to Walter, the return on investment of this one marketing concept has been off the charts. And in case you were wondering, the briefcases are usually returned with a check and a signed contract.

I have spoken with Walter on several occasions about his marketing strategies. I have also read his great book *The Million Dollar Total Business Transformation*, which I highly recommend. He was fortunate to receive wonderful marketing advice from Dan Kennedy, Bill Glazer, and Lee Milteer.

Borrowing ideas and modeling them is not theft, and it is not new. You will see some great ideas in the marketplace in some very unlikely places. When you see something that works in another industry, you have to say, **HOW CAN I APPLY THAT TO MY**

BUSINESS? Get rid of closed-minded thinking that says you can't do it because your business is different. Always think about how something can be changed, tweaked, altered, or adjusted so it *does* fit your business.

It is very dangerous to convince yourself that your business is different. You must realize that <u>no business is different</u>. And the goal of an advisor's business is to acquire clients and keep them for a very long time!

Don't limit your search for innovative marketing ideas to what other financial advisors are doing. Stay focused on what is going on at the local car wash, the chiropractor's office, the dentist's office, the ice cream shop, the dry cleaners, and more. You never know where your next great marketing idea will come from.

YOU GOTTA DO STUFF!

I want to borrow a page from Bill Glazer's playbook. For those of you unfamiliar with the name, he is one of the most celebrated marketing experts in the country and a student of the legendary Dan Kennedy.

Most advisors I know have never advertised their practice in any meaningful way and have little experience in that area. For our purposes, I will use an unusually broad definition of *advertising*. When I have asked FAs point blank how much time they spend on marketing, advertising, or PR each week, the answer is normally **none.**

In Bill's book ***Outrageous Advertising That's Outrageously Successful: Created for the 99% of Small Business Owners Who Are Dissatisfied with the Results They Get,*** he explains that in order to stand out, you must be outrageous and different. He is careful to explain that you are not *necessarily* better, but you are perceived differently by your target prospects, <u>and that difference</u> makes all the difference!

Bill goes on to frame the issue something like this: There are tens of thousands of potential clients out there who can be doing business with you, but they don't know who you are and have never heard of you. So how are you going to solve that problem? Bill's advice? You need to **get noticed**, and the way you do that is to **be creative, innovative, and outrageous.** In other words, you gotta do stuff, *and the more outrageous it is*, the better.

Bill's approach to advertising will challenge you. Your advertising won't look like everyone else's. People will tell you you're being unprofessional. Your messaging won't fit the mold. It's ugly, unprofessional, and weird. **And** that is precisely why you want to incorporate it into your marketing. <u>The concept is to stand out in a crowded marketplace.</u> If your marketing looks like every other financial advisor, the results will be the same as everyone else's—probably *not* very good.

The majority of advisors won't act on this information or even spend $20 to buy Bill's book. So be it. The book is better than a $1,000 two-day marketing course, but then again, you probably didn't sign up for that either. By the way, Bill's second book is even better than his first. It's called *Outrageous Multi-Step Marketing Campaigns That Are Outrageously Successful.* <u>It is a master's level course in marketing.</u>

So if you won't consider being outrageous but still want to move the needle on your business, what about executing a unique idea that has the potential to get your name known far and wide? Sit up and pay attention! *Class is in session.*

HYPOTHETICAL, AMAZING ADVISOR

How many financial advisors do you suppose have sat down and researched a list of 200 radio stations in a 100-mile radius around their office? How many of them have called each one, offering to engage in an interview about a hot retirement strategy, college funding, or a financial topic that is making headlines in the media? Or perhaps they have offered to comment on current legislation such as the SECURE Act that will spell the near death of the stretch IRA?

If our hypothetical advisor were to <u>call one station</u> in the morning and <u>one</u> in the afternoon for 90 days straight, they would have made 180 outgoing calls. Odds are they would have learned something about how to get through to the program managers, news directors, and other decision-makers.

Assuming they were able to book several interviews over three months of calling, they might offer listeners their new book or a free special report they've written on retirement investing. What if our smiling and dialing advisor were to rotate the strategy and make outgoing calls to all those radio stations each and every quarter, offering to discuss different topics each time? Do you suppose they might end up on a program manager's or news director's contact list when a station is in need of a knowledgeable financial type to interview?

Hmm, let's check some of the numbers: 700 to 800 outgoing calls over the course of a year; that's two a day. Do you think you could get pretty good at this with that much practice? If I play the odds, I have to believe that you will get at least a couple of shots at being on the air and have hundreds, if not thousands, of people hearing you, your message, and your name for the first time. Some of those may request your special report, and you will drop them into your lead funnel so you can communicate with them and drip on them over a period of time.

Enhance your opportunity by offering a free special report that is highlighted on the station's website. **You must ask** for this since stations will seldom offer it. By the way, the next time you plan a trip anywhere, contact some local radio stations at your destination ahead of time and offer unique and timely interview material. There's no rule that radio time has to be a local affair. After all, you can have clients all over the country.

WHAT ABOUT REFERRALS?

If you've been paying attention, you are aware that I have focused on the idea that **many financial advisors are lousy marketers**.

No, I didn't read that in a survey or industry journal. I came to the conclusion by asking scores of advisors what they do to market their practices. The question is generally met with an uncomfortable silence. As I alluded to previously, the advisors I spoke with recognize that they *should* be marketing and know it's a good idea. They just don't. It's kind of like knowing it's a good idea to eat your green vegetables, but you don't.

This reluctance appears no different then advisors' unwillingness to **ask for referrals**. Sure, referrals trickle in now and then, but more often than not, FAs have not *installed* a *referral system* in their practice. Notice, I used the words *installed* and *system*—and for good reason. Most advisors default to one-off attempts at referrals, merely asking instead of **installing a referral operating system**.

Any referral operating system is better than NO referral operating system.

It's not my intent to teach referrals 101 here. It's more like taking a *wet hen* into the middle of the living room for all to see and asking who belongs to this sorry looking animal. The lack of a referral system is the wet hen. That said, I will provide one idea that you might consider.

Whatever system you feel is appropriate for your business, practice it. Refine it. Use it. Tweak it. Install it. Live it. Notice I'm not asking what system you feel comfortable with, because *if you were comfortable with any system, you would already be using it.* Remember, growth does not occur in comfort zones, and we know it is uncomfortable for many of us to ask for referrals.

There are dozens of ways to market your practice. I can give examples and suggestions, but you have to choose at least one and implement it. This is about **implementation and execution.**

Here is an example of a simple yet straightforward message you can use. If you did nothing more than end each client review call with something like the conversation below, it would be better than no referral message at all. Change it, improve it, make it yours, but *use something.*

Mrs. Smith, I hope today's review was helpful and gave you a better understanding of your portfolio, how your assets are allocated, and how we have designed it for growth of income in retirement. If there is anyone you care about who might benefit from this type of comprehensive portfolio evaluation, please share your experience with them. It's important that you understand that anyone you recommend to us will be treated with the same professionalism, courtesy, and confidentiality that you have come to expect from our team.

You may also want to let your client know that you have a package of information you can send out to him or her that will provide some information on your team.

As you can see, this is not a complex message. But it can be the beginning of a <u>system</u> if you use it <u>consistently</u>. As I have written previously, you want to create many open doors for prospects to walk through. Consider this idea another door.

Want a little more fire power? How about sending a follow-up letter or e-mail to that client. Repeat important points from your review call and end with the above referral message and instructions on what to do next.

I hope I gave you some thoughts to chew on.

A Failure to Survive

· · · · · · · ·

Make Marketing the Lifeblood of Your Practice

Marketing is often viewed as a mysterious but necessary evil, as in "It's definitely not the business, it's something I have to soil myself with in order to make my business work."

—**Dan Kennedy,** *Master Direct Response Marketer*

AT 330-PLUS YEARS old, European insurer *Lloyd's of London* has been in business longer than most any other company I'm aware of. While there are many factors responsible for its amazing longevity, we will not be speaking of them today. I'm not sure if the following is a holdover from their humble birth in a coffee house *circa 1688* or if it came about later, but the company has a very peculiar way of framing discussions regarding *death*.

Should you speak with a representative of Lloyd's regarding someone's passing, odds are they may refer to the situation as *a failure to survive.* I for one find this fascinating. In fact, I am quite familiar with many financial planning and advisory practices that have experienced a similar failure to survive. In other words, they died. They shut their doors. Sold the furniture. They went OUT OF BUSINESS.

There are many reasons why a practice may shut its doors. Off the top of my head, five reasons come to mind:

- The inability of partners to continue working together
- The inability to control expenses
- Running afoul of laws and regulations
- Poor planning and execution
- **Lack of intelligent marketing**

YOUR LIFEBLOOD—EFFECTIVE MARKETING

I'm sure by now you have figured out that I will discuss the last one on the list. It seems that **effective marketing** is often the lifeblood of a business, whether it is shoe repair, construction equipment rental, or financial planning. Contrary to what some might believe, hoisting a sign above the front door is not marketing; neither is changing your logo (really, folks, people don't give a damn about your logo).

Marketing is what you do to get folks interested in sitting down and talking with you, and sometimes it can be quite complex. Easy sales, like a newspaper or a pack of mints, may or may not require extensive marketing campaigns. However, if you are figuring out the lifetime value of a multi-million-dollar client and come to the conclusion that it is north of $50,000 to $100,000, well, then, your marketing may very well need to be well thought out and comprehensive.

Some of the best marketing advice I ever received was from an extremely successful advisor in Pennsylvania who told me to *"develop a system with LOTS of touches."*

He went on to explain that he has a marketing sequence to get people into a seminar room. He has another sequence for those who *raised their hands*, one for those who accepted an invitation to a personal planning session, and even one for those who failed to show up. He shared with me 12 distinct multi-touch follow-up sequences. These sequences made up his marketing system.

You could look at this and say, "That's too much; who has time to put all these *systems* in place?" He would smile and remind you that **all wealth is built on systems**. Think Ford, McDonald's, Walmart. And by the way, his personal income tops $2.5 million a year, so he might be on to something.

Because his marketing is so successful, he can afford to spend more money to attract his perfect client ($2 million to $5 million in investable assets). He understands that *trust is the currency of the affluent*, and he continually provides relevant information to attract, convert, and retain clients. He is crushing his local competition that floods the market with postcards offering free chicken dinners and a PowerPoint presentation.

He recognizes that he is in the marketing business. He can hire extra CFP™ help anytime to produce additional financial plans. He also understands that *the wealth is in the marketing, not the doing.*

TESTING, TESTING

While attending a marketing conference in San Jose, I wrote in my journal something I knew was true, but I had never spent much time thinking about it. I wrote this:

With whatever I do, I will always have an outcome. It may not be the outcome I wish, but there will always be an outcome. In order to adjust my outcome, I must TEST, tweak, TEST, adjust, TEST, change it up, **TEST***.*

Marketing is all about connection. Whatever your strategy and tactics, you must ask yourself this: *Is what I am doing establishing or facilitating a connection?* If the answer is no, then STOP! Tweak it, change it, adjust it, or start again. Think for a moment. Have you ever tested one marketing idea against another? Why not?

It seems that competitive forces in our industry are almost mandating that you be more creative than ever when attracting and converting clients to your practice. Testing different ideas and then figuring out what works best is essential.

Remember, prospects have more alternatives today than at any time in recent memory. Twenty years ago, I didn't even think about online investment and financial planning, yet today's options include companies such as Betterment, Nerd Wallet, Personal Capital, Mint, and others. Not a week goes by that I'm not hearing or reading about *the death of the full-service financial advisor.*

The financial services industry has undergone massive changes, driven mainly by technological advances. Chants of THE END IS NEAR can be heard everywhere. *These changes have and will continue to affect your practice.* There is no need for your services if you are solely pushing products that are cheaper online. Your services and marketing must be <u>highly personal</u>; your clients must understand that you are a necessary and relevant part of their lives.

In order to escape being thought of as a commodity best acquired at the cheapest price, you must adopt practices that give you the ability to overcome the technological tsunami. That means you must acquire the requisite skills, listen to the right people, and use the best marketing methods in order to escape commodity status and remain profitable.

You will vet many strategies to grow your business. <u>But the important thing is to constantly test one idea, one strategy, and one tactic against another and never consider any outcome a failure.</u> Consider it an outcome that can be improved. You got an outcome; it was not the one you were seeking. What can you change to increase the odds of a better outcome?

To drive this point home, let me share a story with you. I was speaking with a very successful direct mail specialist who mails hundreds of thousands of sales letters to prospects each month. He explained that his company constantly tests every part of the direct mail campaign to see how the results can be improved. Here are a few of the variables they tested, one at a time:

- Large mailing envelope vs. normal business envelope
- Colored envelope vs. white envelope
- Font size and style
- Headline A vs. headline B
- Picture vs. no picture on sales letter

You might think some of the details are bizarre. Yet each and every test and change resulted in verifiable different response rates. They methodically tested one version of the mailing against another, over and over. **Important to note:** The reason only one variable is tested at a time is so you know what caused a change in the response. If you adjust multiple variables simultaneously, you won't know which change led to a change in the response. Yes, this is complicated, but more than $10 million in sales appeared to be worth it from this direct mail campaign.

Back to our industry. **Americans will always need skilled providers of our craft, and you need to find an optimal way to inform them that you exist.** You need to tell them that you may, in fact, be the answer to their financial planning and investment challenges.

Insert yourself in your marketing. Be the solution to your prospects' problems. And don't forget to include the best marketing technique—an emotional hook. Facts don't sell. Emotion does. Never market the *thing*; market the *Who*. Oh, and in case you forgot, **the Who is *you*.**

15

My $250,000
Aha Moment

. . . .

Where to Spend Your Money

*The higher the income, the more the person paid
for who they are, rather than what they do.*

—Dan Kennedy

LET ME PAINT you a picture...

I'm in Dallas, Texas, attending my first advanced marketing conference with an organization I recently joined. It was the second day, and I had already taken 18 pages of notes and captured a dozen great ideas I could implement in my practice. I quickly realized **an uncomfortable truth**: I had been in sales for 20 years and *did not know the first thing about marketing*. There was no better place for me to be that weekend than in that conference room, in that hotel, in Dallas, Texas.

This conference *was not for beginners.* Like me, everyone attending left their families at home, got on planes, and rented hotel rooms to be there in Dallas and learn from some of the foremost marketing experts on the planet. The folks sitting at my table were a varied bunch of highly motivated entrepreneurs from various businesses, all very successful. They were there to get better.

- Mitch owned a modest-sized manufacturing company in Kansas and earned about $42,000 per month. He was there to learn how to double that.
- Jonathan ran a direct mail operation out of Indianapolis and earned about $110,000 per month. He was intent on learning how to double that and greater systematize his operations.
- Kendra inherited her father's custom furniture manufacturing company in Boston and earned $200,000 per month. She was intent on tripling that number and took more notes than I did.

This was not a conference for amateurs. *This place—this organization—*was where the best came to get better. In fact, the organization's tag line is *"a membership community of entrepreneurs and business owners who are dedicated to growing their businesses with better marketing."*

A QUESTION OF MATH

So this brings me to a math question. If I presented you with a *widget* and told you that this was a very unique *widget* and that every time you stuck a dollar in it, $5 would come out, how many dollars would you put in it? The obvious answer is that *you would keep putting in dollars for a very long time!*

So keep that in the back of your mind.

The ideas I gathered at the conference were nothing like the marketing made available to financial advisors at my brokerage firm. I understood that the slick corporate-look marketing pieces I was using were, in fact, useless. One thing that was said to me *stuck like peanut butter to the roof of my mouth.*

"You must craft a message that resonates with your target market."

When I reviewed my firm's marketing products through the filter of that sentence, I understood that I must do things differently. *That's when Adam Witty took the stage.*

Adam Witty is the Founder and Chief Executive Officer of Advantage Media Group, a leading publisher of business, motivation, and self-help authors. He was also a student of the marketing organization sponsoring the conference. In other words, he grew up in this place and was as much a student as a product and success story *and* someone whom I could learn from. I turned to a fresh page in my journal and wrote the name **Adam Witty** at the top.

Adam explained that to capture the attention of your ideal prospect, you must speak directly to them in very personal and emotional language. He went on to explain the *Robert Collier Principal* that <u>**you must enter the conversation already going on in the prospect's mind**</u>.

He then compared and contrasted that with examples of corporate advertising department booklets and brochures, including some from competitors in my own industry. His message was that *no matter your industry*—dentist, chiropractor, financial advisor, or auto mechanic—you could write your own book and **establish your authority and expertise**. You can speak directly to your best prospects with a message meticulously crafted for them. The message Adam was sending out resonated with me. I closed my eyes and had an *aha moment.*

His publishing company had programs to help business owners and service professionals write a book that would function as a ***lead generation magnet***. In plain English, the book would serve as the foundation for all marketing and serve as an important source of differentiation. He explained that the book would become an *evergreen marketing asset*—one that could be used for years.

The more I heard, the more I thought this was a great idea. I had written a little in college—short stories and journal entries—but nothing formal. Still, the idea resonated, and when Adam presented a limited time offer to work with his company at a special *conference-only price*, I literally jumped out of my chair, ran to the back of the room, and signed up for the offer.

Nine months later, Advantage Media published my first book: ***Forging Bonds of Steel: How to Build a Successful and Lasting Relationship with Your Financial Advisor***. The book has been responsible for more than $250,000 of income that I can directly trace back to it. Year after year, I give the book away, and year after year, new clients join my practice based on that book and three others I have written.

While Adam's company offers various publishing models as well as a *speak your book* program, I decided to work with their business editor, and I wrote every word myself. I'm glad I did, as I can look anyone in the eye and say **yes, I wrote it, every single word.**

And remember, when you provide a copy of your book to a prospect, you are marketing yourself.

IT'S TIME TO DISCRIMINATE

Just so there is no misunderstanding, let me make myself clear. I want you to discriminate. I want you to *discriminate about which prospects you spend your marketing money on.* The easiest way to go broke in any marketing approach is to spend the same amount on all prospects. **All prospects are not created equal.**

For example, early in my career, I found there was a segment of clients who generated fees of about $1,000 per year, while another segment generated $7,500 to $10,000 per year.

I quickly learned that it made economic sense to spend more on attracting higher-value prospective clients than on those who would generate a smaller fee. In effect, when I spend marketing dollars, I *discriminate* in favor of prospects who have a higher payoff. And that is exactly what you should be doing.

Let's say you have a list of 600 prospects. While their demographics might be similar—they all live in your county, or maybe they are all homeowners—their psychographics may be quite different. Imagine for a moment how far you can drill down into portions of your list based on spending patterns, hobbies, values, or buying habits.

What if you were to target anyone who bought fine wines, or maybe hunters, golfers, classic car collectors, corporate executives, or people who frequent elegant restaurants? And what if you segmented that list into smaller parts and focused your marketing resources unequally based on their psychographic profiles?

What if you were to create a multistep, multimedia mailing that targets food aficionados who are also golfers? And what if you offered them an exclusive cooking experience at a local golf course with a well-known chef? Or what if you made it a *bring-a-friend event?*

You will want to spend the majority of your marketing dollars on communicating with the affluent. Marketing only to them and establishing account minimums of $500,000, $750,000, or even $1 million will *allow you to change your math.*

What does this mean? It means you can spend a lot more money marketing to these individuals because their lifetime value is significantly higher than other clients. The value of just one $3-million client over a 7- to 10-year period may be $150,000 to $300,000 or more. The math for a $10 million is even more interesting!

You can afford to be generous with your marketing resources when you target these individuals because they have a high LCV—*lifetime client value.* Spending $500 or even $1,000 or more to market to these prospects should be a straightforward business decision governed by math. And that might be an excellent business decision.

Are you spending your marketing dollars equally? Then you may well go broke and curse the day you started marketing. Make the intelligent decision to weight your marketing dollars. Spend them on prospects with a high LCV, and always, **always segment your prospect list**. Remember, prospects are not created equal, and you must factor that into your marketing plans.

16

Marketing Assessment

. . . .

How Am I Doing?

*It would never occur to the average financial advisor
to look outside their industry and adopt effective
marketing ideas they might swipe and deploy.*

—Rodger Friedman

IT'S TIME FOR some self-assessment and some evaluations to measure your marketing level. First, let me ask you two hard questions:

♦ What five things are you doing that you shouldn't be doing?
♦ What five things are you *not* doing that you should be doing?

Process-driven marketing revolves around pre-planned and intelligent implementation. It might be time to create your plan—your strategy—for effective marketing.

First, organize, orchestrate, and execute a marketing system that can be implemented consistently in your practice week after week, month after month.

Then establish authority through content-based marketing materials that educate prospects and speak directly to their fears about financial security and future retirement independence. Your job through strategic marketing is to methodically elevate the levels of trust your prospects have for you so they feel comfortable calling and asking if they can speak with you.

Ask yourself this:

♦ Where do I want my business to be in three, five, or seven years?
♦ What actions am I taking?
♦ What staffing decisions am I making?
♦ What marketing methods am I employing?

In other words, what am I doing to grow my assets under management, my financial planning fees, and my revenues?

Will my current actions take me there in the most effective and efficient way?

MARKETING SELF-ASSESSMENT

This self-assessment might help you evaluate where you are and where you should be going.

Indicate next to each of the marketing methods below whether you are using them on a consistent basis for your practice. Then prioritize them. Which one would you implement first, second, third, and so on?

- ☐ Postcards
- ☐ Direct mail letters
- ☐ Podcasts
- ☐ Blogs
- ☐ Newsletters
- ☐ Special reports
- ☐ Webinars or tele-seminars
- ☐ Magazine or newspaper ads
- ☐ Free-standing inserts in local media
- ☐ Seminars
- ☐ Lunch and learns
- ☐ Team sponsorship
- ☐ Talks at local service organizations
- ☐ Talks at local companies
- ☐ Writing a guest column in an association newsletter
- ☐ Reaching out to media and journalists
- ☐ Connections with local Chamber of Commerce
- ☐ Your own radio show
- ☐ Radio interviews
- ☐ Social media
- ☐ Special reports
- ☐ Write books

THE STERN BUT LOVING PARENT

I heard the story once that Kirby Landis, a consultant to the chiropractic industry, often counseled chiropractors to think of themselves as *the Stern but Loving Parent,* one charged with the responsibility to look out for the welfare and best interests of their patients. The *stern* aspect of the description made reference to the fact that admonitions, instructions, and guidance were often not well received or followed.

There seems to be little difference between this and a parent's instruction to their child that Facebook can wait and that they should sit down at the kitchen table and work on the book report due the following week.

Despite the best of intentions and a deep-seated desire to help, both the chiropractor and the parent face a challenging task. And then there's me—your "advisor-parent" when it comes to financial advisor marketing. I've encouraged you to plan, strategize, and set aside time and money in order to market your practice. Deep down inside, I know that some of you won't follow many of the recommendations in this book.

You might be inspired and encouraged by now, but you also might be viewing these ideas and steps like a *cafeteria plan*—you might choose to do this but not that, and this thing here, only if something else comes to pass. But a marketing plan for your practice is not an either-or proposition. The idea is to take *all these ideas, all these actions* and get a desired outcome.

It's time to decide on a marketing plan, commit to carrying it out, and enjoy the results. Many **FAs want the results but aren't willing to put in the work**. Now is the time for *the stern but loving parent— me*—to make an entrance.

We only have so many hours in a day and so many days in our careers. We should not knowingly waste them on "filling small cavities all day" (see Chapter 1) when we could be doing "expensive implants for celebrities." Become the specialist—the **celebrity**—in your field. Market yourself—the **important _who_** in the financial advisor marketplace. **People are willing to pay more** for those who have a specialty and are famous in their niche.

This stern parent is telling you to do this before you create one more spreadsheet, before you put together one more 125–page report that will earn you $1,925. This parent is telling you to differentiate yourself from the other 299,999 financial advisors in the country and start making a large six-figure or even a seven-figure income.

An Unlikely Pair

. . . .

The Merger of Financial Advising and Tech Marketing

The best of the best share many common characteristics.

—**Rodger A. Friedman,** *Forging Bonds of Steel*

WHO ARE YOU HANGING OUT WITH?

As I studied Dan Kennedy's concepts, I found I was in very good company. I looked at who was attending the conferences I was attending, who participated in the conference calls, and who created monster libraries of the same materials I had purchased.

The entrepreneurs who made up this group were some of the most successful people I have ever met. At the low end, some I met earned $35,000 per month. At the high end, I met several who were earning $500,000 per month! This *gathering of minds* was a very comfortable *place* to be. Everywhere around me were really smart individuals who never stopped learning, who asked questions, who took advantage of resources, and who took action and executed. And most gratifying to me was their desire to share their stories, successes, and failures.

One of them stood out to me. His name? **Parthiv Shah**. He wasn't the richest, the tallest or the best spoken. But he *was* friendly and wickedly smart. I met him at a conference several years ago when Dan Kennedy brought him up on stage to address the subject of *implementation*. Since this was an area I needed to improve in, I paid attention and took plenty of notes. I'm glad I did. Afterwards, I made my way to the front to speak with Parthiv.

We spoke for a long while, and I determined that we had both studied many of the same marketing strategies and concepts of Dan Kennedy. To say that Kennedy's ideas were transformative in my business would be an understatement. Parthiv agreed.

Then it dawned on me that Parthiv and I were implementing many of the <u>same strategies</u>—me in the wealth management arena and Parthiv in the digital and direct response marketing and funnel-building arena. And I was delighted to find out that he lived a few towns over from me in Montgomery County, Maryland.

As I came to know Parthiv, I formed a deep respect for his knowledge, expertise, and ability to **implement** what Kennedy was teaching. Along the way, I provided him with insights into wealth building. Oddly enough, we never hired each other or had conversations about becoming each other's client. The wealth level of my clients was a bit higher than Parthiv's investable assets, so I never pursued him as a client.

Over time, I became a prolific copywriter, implementing many of Kennedy's tactics. Likewise, I had successfully created a stable team of freelance virtual assistants to support me in my marketing operations. All the while, I went to Parthiv for many tech answers that were beyond my abilities. I taught Parthiv aspects about money and wealth that had taken decades to internalize, and he taught me more about implementation. *We eventually became friends.*

For years, we spent countless hours in mastermind groups, updating each other on our businesses and personal lives. We just never bothered to bill each other.

SHARING WHAT I'VE LEARNED

This is my fifth book, so it's evident that I like to share what I have learned during my 39-year financial services journey. But I designed all my previous books as lead generation magnets—engineered to be *given* to prospects, centers of influence, and others—to generate additional business. It was never my intention to try for *The New York Times* best seller list or to make a fortune from my writing. My books serve a purpose and reinforce my business. But this book is different.

This book is designed for a different audience—*the professional financial advisor.* I firmly believe that many FAs are not avid readers, astute students of marketing, or prolific copywriters. I also don't believe that many of them get on planes and fly all across the country to attend marketing conferences that have nothing to do with financial planning or wealth management.

While there are many books geared toward marketing, it appears that few were written by FAs who have **designed *and* implemented advanced marketing strategies**. Fewer still have the mindset and sense of urgency to pursue subject matter mastery. I realize that I am not the typical FA since I have literally written hundreds of thousands of words of *copy* that have appeared in articles, special reports, and books.

Plainly stated, FAs are not known to be marketing wizards, either for lack of know-how, a different mindset, or a lack of infrastructure. AND, **this gave me an idea**. When I saw what Parthiv does for attorneys, dentists, doctors, and others, I invited him to collaborate with me and rearticulate my strategies in a systematic way so any financial advisor could use it to grow their own practice.

And that's how we became an unlikely pair of successful entrepreneurs who want to share our knowledge and expertise with *you*, a financial advisor with all kinds of potential!

I invite you to continue reading this book. **And welcome to Part II by Parthiv Shah.**

PART II

The Iceberg You Don't See

ART AND SCIENCE OF
MARKETING MECHANICS

18

The Importance of Systems, Processes, and Rhythms

. . . .

What Separates Good from Great?

Change can be frightening, and the temptation is often to resist it. But change almost always provides opportunities – to learn new things, to rethink tired processes, and to improve the way we work.

—Klaus Schwab

REMEMBER AT THE beginning of this book when I described your practice as an **iceberg**? We talked about the parts of your business that are visible and the parts that are not—the dangerous, hidden unforeseen events. They're hidden from you because you don't have sufficient expertise to identify them. You don't know how to calculate their overall risk. <u>You don't have the tools necessary</u> to get out of harm's way.

That day when Roger and I were at lunch with Greg Banasz of Steward Partners Global Advisory, we devised a process and sketched out what we should include in this book in order to create value for you. It took several hours. Some of it was scribbling the overall concept, and some of it was revising and preparing exactly what the book should include. Immediately after lunch, we sketched it out on a whiteboard to dissect our thoughts, add to them, and remove what was superfluous.

Over the course of many hours of deep thought, mind mapping, and documenting our scattered and disorganized notes, we succeeded in a rough format for our book project. Our intent was to create a logical chain of action for advisors in the financial services industry, and we worked hard to get it right. I believe with all my heart that we did.

At that lunch, I explained **Magnetic Marketing** to Greg. That was the first time he had heard that phrase, but once I explained the concept, he said, "But that's what we have been doing from the beginning of time." Rodger and I looked at each other and smiled. "Yep." said Rodger. "Greg, what you and I know as the right thing to do in our business is described as a marketing concept in a book by renowned author **Dan Kennedy.**

Magnetic Marketing Dan Kennedy coined the term **Magnetic Marketing** decades ago. The concept has also been described by other marketing theorists using different words, phrases, and infographics. Infusionsoft calls this concept a "Lifecycle Marketing Planner." Hubspot calls it "inbound marketing." Digital Marketer calls it "Customer Value Optimization and Value Journey Canvas."

In my book ***Business Kamasutra***, I drew parallels between how humans take their personal relationship from persuasion to pleasure, and how the principles of relationships in humanity can be applied to any business.

In reality, it is all **one system**, and every successful financial advisor has been following that system to a certain degree. You need to find prospects who are the right fit for you. Your ideal prospect has the needs you can solve. Your ideal prospect will be attracted to you because you can figure out their problems and enrich their life. Your ideal prospect will trust you, be compliant with your process, be grateful for the results you bring to them, become your best friend and advocate in the community, and overtly introduce you to their sphere of influence. Your ideal prospect will eventually become your ideal client who will <u>pay, stay, and refer</u>.

YOUR BUSINESS ICEBERG

Imagine you are on the infamous cruise ship *Titanic*. Your business happens to be the ship, and you are the captain commanding the helm. You have vast leadership experience. After all, you're a *business owner* who is running all the day-to-day tasks and duties that keep you and your family clothed, sheltered, and fed. But back to your iceberg story.

Your initial passengers signed up for this maiden voyage in the "unsinkable" *Titanic*. They were worry-free and looking forward for an incident-free jaunt across the seas to America. At first, all is well. The crew and the leaders are the pride of the guests.

As your *Titanic* (your financial advisory practice) is steaming along on the surface of the ocean, you spot an iceberg in the distance. At first, the sighting appears insignificant, although it is much closer than it appears. As you approach the obstacle, the size and scope of the floating obstruction become a worrisome nuisance that you cannot ignore.

However, your faith in the training the crew embodies will carry the day. Even though you believe your new ship is a sound one, you become apprehensive. You go directly into crisis management mode to steer away from this dangerous, floating menace. You spin the wheel as far to the left as possible, shouting orders, halting the engines, but all is for naught. The ship strikes the frozen and submerged ocean threat. The famous luxury liner begins to take on water.

The passengers are overcome with fear and pray for their lives to be spared somehow. Some passengers can sense the ill-fated nature of the encounter, and they panick. Others calmly dance to the onboard quartet, seemingly unconcerned about the panic and dismay around them. Panic and denial—both can be hazardous to your health.

You did what your training had instilled in you—the keen ability to avoid visible dangers. Your inflated confidence in the ship and its crew was shortsighted.

We know from the real *Titanic* that most of the incomprehensible mass of the iceberg lies beneath the surface, hidden but supporting the visible edifice. The ship's strong hull and the hidden, frozen, dangerous, floating mountain are not meant to be combatants. When those two forces collide, there is only one winner.

What you failed to realize is that what is visible *is not* the entire iceberg. What lies beneath the surface of the water is where the real danger lies.

And so it is with business. Most business owners suffer the same illusion as the *Titanic*'s captain and crew did (please tell me you know of the hidden dangers within your business).

You know the rest of the story. The huge ship capsizes and sinks. The passengers and crew fill up what lifeboats are available with terrified women, children, and men. You also know about all the lives that were lost. As captain of your ship, it's your responsibility to have successful voyages. The ones that end badly are also your responsibility. Do you want your destiny to be hitting icebergs head-on in the middle of the night? Or do you want to navigate calmly around them? Do you want to be good, or do you want to be great?

What separates good from great in your business? The answer is single-mindedness and leadership. Systems, processes, and rhythms are also *critical* to the elements of business. Processes are all the parts and pieces found within a system that create the functionality of whatever the deliverable may be. Rhythms—communication rhythms that provide steady and consistent workflows from disparate groups to a singular voice—require thought and consideration.

DIRECT RESPONSE MARKETING

Within the field of marketing, there is a discipline called **direct response marketing**. That discipline encourages a **response** from the prospect and an **engagement or conversation** before the prospect is ready to do business with you. In this discipline, the marketer approaches the prospect with a gift or a useful resource that can help the prospect. If the prospect is interested in the gift, the prospect **responds** to the marketing effort and asks for the gift. This initial exchange of gift between marketer and prospect starts a conversation and an engagement that goes from acquaintance to temporary suspension of disbelief, to trust, to an initial transaction, to a friendship, to **a business relationship**. If a relationship is built this way, it is meant to be, and it usually lasts a very long time.

Direct response marketing relies on a steady flow of communication in various formats (print, audio, video) for both internal and external stakeholders, as well as prospective clients.

STRATEGIC MARKETING PLAN

Perhaps the most important foundation for your processes and systems is your **strategic marketing plan**. Mapping out exactly the steps you will take to ensure your magnetic attraction machine is operating at maximum efficiency means the difference between sailing across the Atlantic in a luxury liner or a fishing trawler.

At eLaunchers, we live and die by systems, processes, and rhythms. Everything we do is to bring the communications flow into the correct rhythm, voice, tone, and cadence for engagement, endearment, attraction, retention, and advocacy. We'll cover in this book the various components of what we do on an individual client level. From that, you, the reader, can become inspired to adopt a similar system of automated and clockwork precision in your prospect attraction methods.

There is a system that ultimately **converts a lead to a client**. It starts with prospect attraction and goes to lead acquisition, education, nurturing, relationship building, and, ultimately, conversion.

In the financial advisory and wealth management spheres, the opening conversation starts with a helping hand from the advisor, who is the expert in the field. The prospect needs help because the field of wealth management is confusing and frightening. There are too many options. Most options are inappropriate, and investors are scared because they don't know what to do and are well aware that they are underqualified to make mission-critical decisions to protect and grow their nest egg. They know how to make money, they have discipline to not spend the money, and they deposit the money in an account they will not touch. But that's where their ability ends. Here is the most common question every consumer asks: **"Now what do I do?"**

THE FINANCIAL ADVISOR AND THE PROSPECT

We believe that **every household in America can benefit from working with a financial advisor.** Not everyone can afford one, and not everyone who can afford one realizes they need help. We need to first find prospects who could benefit from our services and will cheerfully pay for the engagement and fully participate in our process. Once we find such a prospect, we need to make them aware of the problem in their life and position ourselves as the solution to that problem. We need to show them that having a meaningful conversation with us about their personal finances is the prudent thing to do.

Our goal is for a client to raise their hand and say, *"Yes, I am ready to take the necessary steps to place my assets under management with you."*

But the systems and processes don't stop there. To keep the client enthralled with the services you provide, you—the financial advisor marketer—must believe in your heart of hearts that this client is the most valuable asset you possess. It's not the initial financial planning or investment management fee that is important. It's the lifetime value that the client represents. Rodger discussed this at length in Part I of this book.

Knowing the client is a long-term, *income-producing asset* under your guidance and management takes thought, strategy, and implementation. You want to keep the client pleased to the point where they become your invisible sales force. We'll talk about retention systems and processes later in the book, so don't worry about knowing everything there is to know about that right now.

19

Why We Compare Your Marketing and Sales to an Iceberg

· · · · · · ·

Is Your Business Titanic II?

I describe the design process as like the tip of the iceberg. What you don't see is the long haul: all the endless auditing and things like that.

—**Norman Foster**

AT THE BEGINNING of this book, we talked about the infamous *Titanic* and its floating nemesis—**the iceberg**. The story makes for a fine example to teach the system of the Purchaser's Continuum, also known as the Buyer's Journey. What you don't want is a catastrophe where you not only lose precious clients (passengers on the sinking ship) but also your business (the ship).

It dawned on Rodger and me that an iceberg is much like a

business. Some aspects of it can be seen quite easily, but much of it cannot be seen, or it can be ignored due to the hectic nature of our business lives. Think of it as working **in** your business versus working **on** your business.

THE ICEBERG – THE VISIBLE AND THE HIDDEN

An iceberg represents the visible and hidden elements of a business. An iceberg is much like a *marketing funnel*. There is a top, a middle, and a bottom. In marketing language, the prospect attraction, the generation process, and the systems are the Top of the Funnel (**TOFU**), the Middle of the Funnel (**MOFU**), and the Bottom of the Funnel (**BOFU**).

The TOFU is visible with prospects of all kinds entering our continuum. The business world moves at a much quicker pace than it did 20 or 30 years ago. But regardless of then or now, automation today is a tool very much in demand for just about all occupations. Marketing automation is especially efficient since a person or company's messaging to the marketplace (exterior) for prospect attraction occurs whether you're in the office or not. Internal marketing efficiency performs an equally important set of tasks to nurture, inform, educate, and even entertain your existing clients.

Internal marketing using automation can even create client ascension through add-on products or services, upselling, or even creating VIP continuity opportunities to build AUM. Automation can also be utilized to re-engage former clients, encourage referrals, and build advocacy.

SOME LEVEL OF RISK

Like a ship on the ocean, there is always some level of risk. If your business is built on a cluster of fractured bits and pieces or on partial builder's plans, there could be trouble on the high seas, creating chaos and risk escalation.

I am positive that you don't want to end up floating on a door in the middle of the ocean in winter, praying for a rescue that you fear won't come in time. I'm certain that there are insufficient lifeboats, but a string quartet calmly playing to keep everyone calm is not available. If you are no good at navigation, your practice just might become *Titanic II*.

I'll explain this more in the next chapter and spell out what is visible on the surface of a financial advisor's "ocean" and what is hidden from sight.

We at eLaunchers refer to the visible tools and tactics as external marketing. Yes, there is more to it besides marketing to the world; there's internal marketing as well. We'll get to what you should be doing internally after a review of all the things you should already be doing and monitoring. The online marketing you might be doing and the offline marketing you are allowed to do are what need discussion. Everything you have already read in this book was in preparation for the next important chapters.

THE ANATOMY OF YOUR MARKETING ICEBERG

Your marketing "iceberg" is a complex being that must be understood in order for it to be seen and not sink your ship.

There is a particular anatomy of your marketing iceberg. Imagine the iceberg with elements above the water's surface and the rest not immediately in view.

TRAFFIC

Let's look at some elements of your marketing iceberg. The first element is **Traffic**—prospects coming to your various online and offline contact points.

- **Digitally Generated Traffic** comes from places such as digital ads, social media posts, your website, and landing pages you've set up. It can also be e-mails that direct prospects and clients to downloadable educational marketing materials such as e-books, digital newsletters, special reports, checklists, and a litany of other marketing assets to attract prospects and leads.
- **Offline Traffic** is generated by tactics such as direct response marketing, direct mail, press releases, and print media such as newspapers, magazines, flyers, postcards, and newsletters. It can include billboards, live presentations, speeches, events such as local community and social events, social cause activities, and other display media that are not online.
- **Referral Traffic** is the result of your spheres of influence. It might come from CPAs or attorneys referring their friends, family, or associates, or it may be due to your gentle encouragement and solicitation.
- **Top of the Funnel** is produced primarily by your website, blogs, landing pages, and downloads. It's all the online and offline ways to attract prospects and leads and request more information.
- **Middle of the Funnel** is part of the marketing cycle that

comes into play from the initial contact through the decision-making action. That is where prospects and leads become more familiar with your offerings, learn more about your firm, special offerings, additional education, information, and specific downloads. At this level, there is some normal attrition as timing, interest, or suitability no longer match the prospect's level of interest.

◆ **Bottom of the Funnel** is when the sales cycle occurs, from the moment of the first interview through the funding of accounts.

◆ **Post-Close** includes multiple activities at this point in the client's journey.

◆ **Ascension** means increasing the overall AUM volume through various actions such as establishing a comprehensive referral program.

◆ **Retention** is the area where small business owners typically fall short. There are several strategies to accomplish extending the lifetime client value for as long as possible.

◆ **Advocacy** is when, through consistent management of your retention program and communications carefully designed to elevate the perceptions of clients, some will naturally grow to the level of a raving fan, advocating on your behalf.

There are visible and hidden components to an iceberg—and there are visible and hidden components to your marketing. There's online and offline marketing as well as internal and external marketing. Some are visible, and some are not so visible.

I briefly mentioned TOFU (**top of funnel**), MOFU (**middle of funnel**), and BOFU (**bottom of funnel**) as elements of the Buyer's Journey or Purchaser's Continuum. Marketers came up with this visual representation to try to make it easier to understand. As a marketer, I get it, and I hope you do as well. If not, there are plenty of examples and explanations on the Internet. Picture a funnel with a variety of people who are interested in learning about your financial advisory, retirement planning, or education funding solutions. They may have come from any of your lead-generating efforts online or offline.

They will travel from the TOFU through the MOFU and hopefully through the BOFU. At each stage along the way, you share nurturing educational information with them, but some of them may decide to stay at a spot that is comfortable for them. Maybe they aren't ready to commit to anything just yet. Some may leave the funnel for any number of reasons. As prospects travel down, the funnel gets narrower as fewer prospects make decisions. That's self-elected attrition, which is fine. Perhaps they aren't your ideal prospect after all, or perhaps they have shifted their focus somewhere else.

We've touched briefly on the concerns you should be able to see above the proverbial surface of the ocean you call your practice. Let's look at these topics in more detail in the upcoming chapters.

The Top of the Iceberg

. . . .

Everything Visible

I will love the light for it shows me the way, yet I will endure the darkness because it shows me the stars.

—Og Mandino

ABOVE THE OCEAN'S surface, your view of the upper part of the iceberg is unblocked. You see your floating danger clearly and focus on it. You also see what's around it and what's on the water's surface. And yes, we know there's something underneath the water that's not readily visible, where some of the real danger lies. We'll get to that, so please stay with me. But first, let's look at everything visible—the top of the iceberg. Here's what you can see as you market your business.

EVERYTHING VISIBLE

Direct Mail – Often thought of as passé, direct mail is one of the only media vehicles that has a nearly 100% open rate. As for information privacy, direct mail is perhaps the only *privacy-assured* way to share marketing messages. The envelope carries a message that cannot be seen by prying eyes.

Regulations are constantly being expanded to certain protected and unprotected groups. Recently, the United Kingdom ruled it against the law to use images that portray gender-specific roles. Picturing a man playing catch with his son is now illegal since it allows the viewer to believe that women are inferior in that activity. Yes, truth is stranger than fiction. But direct response marketing by mail is alive and well.

Published Works – Have you written a book? How about three? Five? More? None? Writing a book is one of the best ways to increase your credibility, authority, and assumed celebrity. Imagine calling on a prospective client and presenting her or him with a book on the pertinent topic with your name as the author. What do you think that could do for your chances of securing that prospect? While there are no guarantees in life, you might have a fighting chance to win over the competition because you "wrote the book on it"—and that can go a long way.

Experts in social psychology and human behavior have said that out of six people in a group, there is usually one person who seems to command the most attention.

How do you rank in terms of perceived authority? Are you the leader people look up to? Do they hang on your every word? Or are you the one sheepishly listening without even breathing loudly for fear of being noticed? A book or an active speaking schedule are some of the best ways to grow your audience, expand your brand, and increase your credibility and celebrity.

Community Involvement – In your local community, do you stand out as an "almost-celebrity," or are you merely a financial advisor or the owner of a financial advisory service firm? How do you stand out from all the others like you in your marketplace?

When you are out in public, do people know who you are? Do they value you as an integral part of the fabric of the town? Or are you just one of the myriad financial and wealth advisors who populate the area? Does anyone care if you even exist? These are all questions designed to get you to think about your most important asset—*your reputation.*

Being actively involved with the community automatically affects your offline reputation. Remember, you're always being watched. I don't mean you're under scrutiny, but in some ways, you are.

If you are a member of the Chamber of Commerce, the Lion's Club, the Rotary Club, or the dozens of other civic groups in nearly every community, you're being noticed. How do you present yourself at these and other public gatherings?

These are great places to build a reputation, a good way to build trust, build relationships, and become known as the local expert. Participating in the activities that are always going on at one organization or another is one of the best ways to grow your offline presence in your local area.

The excuse that *"I live in a big city"* won't fly. Why not? Because big cities are comprised of smaller, local communities within the metro area. And the suburbs are all small communities of different sizes. Chances are you're a resident of the suburbs, but regardless, where you live *is a community.* **Make your presence known.** Go the extra mile and get involved. The *"I don't have time"* excuse is perhaps the lamest one of all. We all get the same 24 hours every day. It's what you do with them that makes all the difference.

Events – It's all well and good to make a financial donation to the local charities. Actively participating as an officer or sponsor of charity events is one of the best ways to build instant credibility. Those with like-minded interests in humanitarian efforts notice each other, especially the up-and-comers and the established upper-class residents.

What better way to build a business than being accepted into the sphere of influence that is much larger than yours is presently. It's not who you know but who knows you. Wealthy people are careful with who they affiliate with. They often will take a suggestion from a member of their social network over an advertisement, so getting within their sphere of influence builds your credibility. It's the same in business—trust comes from knowing, liking, and respecting their peers. Become one.

At eLaunchers, we also give back to our society. We actively support the Make-a-Wish Foundation. We are also actively involved with Montgomery College where we assist college students through paid internships.

Industry Events – Opportunities to either build or damage a reputation are not limited to online or offline sources. Industry events such as workshops, conferences, and conventions are ripe with opportunities to shine. The occasional gatherings with your peers are great opportunities to share insights, tips, tricks, and even hacks, if you will. No one knows everything. We learn from others, so why not share some nuggets that are not common knowledge? If you are a well-read individual (which you should be), you might come across a bit of news, some pending legislation, or some nugget of what's happening in your industry that may not be common knowledge. Sharing that information with fellow advisors and asset managers helps build your respect in the industry. One day, that might turn into a referral. Who knows?

Business Cards – Here's a question you probably haven't considered much. How many business cards do you print at one time? 500? 1,000? More? And how many times in one year do you have to reprint them? Once? Twice? More? Let's say that you order cards by the thousand and reprint them one time per year. That's 1,000 business cards per year. How long have you been a financial advisor? Ten years or longer? For the sake of easy math, let's assume 10 years. That's 10,000 cards in circulation. The question is this: How many of those cards are still part of people's lives?

Even if you are fortunate enough to secure only 1% of those as clients, that's a hundred clients in 10 years. One hundred cards are in people's wallet or on their desks. You have a place in the lives of 100 people and their families. That's 100 people who know, like, trust, and respect you with their life savings, their investments, their retirement incomes, their lifestyles. One hundred clients in 10 years is a whole lot of clients, especially when you're handling their fortunes. Do you track every card and who you handed them to? That's unlikely.

Where are the other 9,900 business cards? They are probably in a landfill or recycling facility. Thank goodness they don't cost that much.

One more question to wrap up this section. Have you secured a tenth of 1% of every business card you've ever had printed? Think about that for a while.

Referral Traffic – Let's say your prospect "raised their hand." They built up sufficient trust and knowledge, and now they are a client. Hooray! They agreed to let you serve them. They have entrusted their assets to you for safeguarding and growth.

Trust is there, and respect and advocacy are in place. So why not gently work on an ongoing referral system? I don't mean to browbeat your valuable clients, but I am encouraging an occasional, well-thought-out referral campaign that is specifically geared to softly nudge your clients to introduce their friends and associates to your firm. It doesn't have to be a one-and-done. There are discreet methods of establishing and maintaining an open referral program, one you can occasionally mention at appropriate times.

An active referral campaign is one of the best investments you can make in order to add new clients. Your clients have placed their trust in you. They want you to not allow the markets, regulations, or decision-making on investment choices erode their retirement accounts and investment assets. It's up to you to follow through on everything you have ever told them. You owe them at least that much.

You also owe them ongoing communication. No one likes to live in a vacuum. People need to be reassured, informed, encouraged, and educated. That's what we call *internal marketing*.

Because you have done such a fabulous job nurturing them, rewarding them, and making them feel ultra-special, your clients have become your invisible sales force. If your existing clients refer prospects to you, the trust barrier is almost eliminated. Most referrals will gladly join your community of clients because you have already cultivated an atmosphere of trust. Advocacy is a very powerful tool in your toolkit, and it pays huge dividends because there is so little acquisition cost.

Former clients should not be counted out. Just because they have left your firm (unless it was on negative terms) doesn't mean they won't consider returning. There is always an opportunity to bring them back into the business. It's what we call a *reactivation campaign.* Again, this is not a hard sell by any means. It's professional, discreet, and gentle.

YOUR ACTIONS SPEAK VOLUMES

What you do speaks volumes. It's the e-mail sequences, the print newsletters mailed to their home, the ongoing "unexpected extras" like cards sent to mark important dates (birthday, anniversary, kid's graduation, etc.). But that is just the tip of the proverbial iceberg. What else can you do to maintain and improve the relationships you have with your existing clients?

What about **occasional small tokens of appreciation** delivered to their home or office (home is better) from time to time. Here's a secret to keeping track of this: schedule something for every month (except the major holidays at the end of the year), and make it appear random. How? Pre-planned and distributable unexpected extras for a different day of the month every month. Your clients will forever be surprised when the package arrives one month on the 7th and the next month on the 13th, 24th, 29th, or any day of your choosing. Just make it appear to be random. And *include a handwritten note* thanking them for the faith and trust they've placed in you.

Because you and your client are expecting a long-term relationship, you should **become familiar with their family.** Make a file with family members' names and birthdays. Include your client's favorite musicians, authors, sweets, and beverages. Anything can be added as their favorites. That way, you can make these "random" gifts specifically for them as individuals, not a mass-produced gift everyone gets. Take time to personalize every transaction you have with your clients.

I realize that some laws prevent certain acts of generosity. You cannot pay for a referral, so how can you say thank you once the referred person joins your firm?

CAUTION: Don't even consider sending logo merchandise. People don't want to advertise your firm. They'd rather have their name on something at home for guests to see. It might be a piece of crystal, a monogrammed throw blanket, a scarf, an engraved photo frame, and more.

How about an annual (or semi-annual) client open house? You can have it at your office and do it up to show off your digs. Create formal invitations, RSVP return cards, and follow-up letters or notes to let them know how much fun they'll have. Since people aren't so good at responding by mail, be sure to allow them to call or e-mail to accept the invitation.

And as long as you are throwing a celebration, ask your clients to bring a guest or two. With the invitation, include a mini invitation to the affair for their guests. And think about it—it's a referral card of sorts.

Keep your clients informed, incentivized, and motivated. There are marketing tools that can automate much of the internal and external marketing communications, and we'll get to that in a bit.

Centers of Influence Referrals – We spoke of community events, charities, Chamber of Commerce, social organizations, and your professional associations—all great places to get referrals. As a well-known professional in all your spheres of influence, it's only natural for others to encourage their friends and associates to meet you. Gentle encouragement and a pleasant request may be all you need to get another client acquisition. I'm confident that if it is structured and carried out consistently, a steady stream of referrals can be yours.

Think about that iceberg again. Your typical vision is focused on what's above the water, that part of your business that contains many things: your website, your blogs, and pillar pages (well-written, long articles). Your iceberg may include supporting articles, client and prospect educational materials, and many other marketing assets. All these assets can not only be seen but managed, improved, and risk-averse. They can produce abundance if managed properly.

In the next chapter, we'll take a close look at these marketing tools—specifically, your online presence—and how you can put them to use.

The Top of The Funnel (TOFU)

Your Internal Marketing Efforts

Instead of one-way interruption, Web marketing is about delivering useful content at just the right moment that a buyer needs it.

—David Meerman Scott

SO WHAT DOES an online presence mean? Online marketing may be social media posts, blog articles, downloadable materials, podcasts, and so forth. These things may or may not occur with regularity. Remember, there is a world of opportunity beyond LinkedIn and Facebook.

Your online presence includes many, many things, but in just a few words, it's a snapshot of who you are, what you do, who you know, and who knows you. And it's also about how you are perceived online.

YOUR ONLINE PRESENCE

Your Website – How does your website represent you? Does it look proportionate on handheld devices? Does it have content and visuals that support your ideal client, or does it speak of you, you, you? Remember, prospective clients search online for reasons unknown. However, most prospects come to your site to find the right person, services, or firm that can solve their concerns and frustrations and help them begin to sleep better at night. Here's what your website should communicate: how you are *THE* solution they have been seeking. There should be videos that are educational and informative and help your prospective client. You can include content in various formats that can be downloaded in exchange for an e-mail address and a first name. It can not only help the prospect but also help you grow a lead list.

Media Presence – There are online press release firms that handle just digital, but there are also those that push press releases to Associated Press International, United Press International, news outlets such as television and radio, and more. Do you appear anywhere in those circles? If so, your celebrity is growing. If not, work at it. There are a host of reasons to seek press coverage, write press releases, and garner media attention. Anything of note that shows up in print media is likely to also show up online.

Pillar Pages – Pillar pages, along with what are known as cluster pages, are a boon to your online presence and authority position. Pillar pages are well-written, detailed long-form articles that can stand alone as a small e-book or essay on a particularly meaningful topic. Cluster pages are also articles, but they are written to go into more detail on certain aspects of the pillar page. Both of these articles can stand on their own. Combined, they add up to great educational material designed to assist the public, especially your ideal prospect. They're just as valuable to your existing clients, so they pull double duty. First, they attract and persuade new prospects. Second, they provide valuable information to keep your existing clients engaged, interested, and more knowledgeable about you and your business.

Your Blog – Blog articles about topics your prospective audience is interested in have multiple benefits. First, <u>consistent communication with your audiences keeps your firm top of mind</u>. That's critical, because usually out of sight is out of mind. Remaining in the limelight with pertinent copy, videos, podcasts, articles, and so forth not only keeps you visible but helps draw ideal audiences closer and closer to you. How many blog posts should you produce per week? That's a tricky question. For some industries, once a month might be acceptable, but most require much more than that. Think for a moment about how often your prospects, clients, and centers of influence like to hear from you. Remember, as a financial advisor, you have many *money topics* to write about. But in the end, I guess it would depend on your audience's interest level. Don't forget, people learn in different ways. Some are auditory, others visual, and still others are kinesthetic. People prefer to hear, watch, and listen. Some like to see, touch, or feel. Your specific audience would benefit from all these styles of marketing communication.

In addition to your website and blog, if you offer a podcast, a video, or even a Facebook live event, you and your firm can pop up there. These are additional marketing assets that help you build awareness and brand image. The world has fallen in love with videos. There has also been extreme interest in listening to informative podcasts while people are driving to and from work—their "drive-time university." Remember, anything you decide to use must have the blessing of your compliance folks. For that reason, you will want to discuss your marketing ideas with them to determine how best to execute them *and* find out if there are any **compliance or legal obstacles** you are unaware of.

Here's another important point to remember. **<u>Just because no one in your firm has used a particular marketing strategy does not mean it can't be done.</u>** It just means you need to work with your compliance folks to determine HOW it can be done while protecting you and your firm.

Guest Blogs – You should consider identifying top influencers in your field of specialty and follow them on social media and their blogs. Frequently commenting will get you noticed, especially if your comment adds to the conversation this person is having with their target audience. Request an opportunity to post a guest blog on your site. And, not to sound like a broken record, but always discuss your plans with the compliance folks to determine what you are allowed to do.

It might take a while to break through to that, but it never hurts to ask. Also, after you think there's been enough dialogue between you and the influencer through blog comments and social postings, see if you can be a guest blogger on their blog site. That's called influence by proxy.

Online Search – Many firms go to great lengths to get to page one on the Google search results. Getting there without ads is possible, but staying on page one is quite another. Search engine optimization (SEO) is a combination of actions that need to be taken daily, or your placement on Google's rankings is likely to falter. Know this: In 2016, Google's Matt Cutts stated that he and his team performed more than 600 algorithm adjustments. We heard about a few of them, but 600 are almost two per day. Fast forward to 2018. Google made a record number of 3,234 algorithm changes as reported by MOZ. Do you think staying on page one is easy?

Your Social Presence – Social media has become the new word of mouth. Posting your blog articles on social media spreads your message far and wide—that is, if it's quality content. Don't fall into the trap of posting substandard blogs. Your reputation depends on quality, not necessarily quantity. Just be consistent. If someone comments on your posts, take the time to respond with a thank you. Some appreciation is in order. Negative commentary, however frustrating and perhaps unjust, should not be left to linger. Always apologize, even if you have absolutely no idea from whom or where the comment originated. There are solutions to spam responses and ill-conceived or out-and-out lies, but that's a topic for another time. Just know that all comments deserve a prompt—and always positive—response.

The more social media sites your ideal audiences hang out on, the more content you should share on each of them. You might never know where a new prospect comes from because someone on a site might have shared your information with someone in need of your services.

But it's just not enough to have a large following on LinkedIn and Facebook. Lots of those connections more than likely came from people requesting a connection for the sole purpose of boosting their notoriety and getting 5,000 or 10,000 connections. How many of them know you? How many of them care about you?

Online Listings – One thing many small business owners and services practitioners often overlook are listing sites. They're easy to ignore because tracking them is very time-consuming. NAP (name, address, phone number) listings are everywhere. That information is pushed out on the Internet by what are known as "aggregators."

There are four main aggregators: Factual, Acxiom, Infogroup, and Localeze. Bots are sent out to search the Web for irregularities with information on companies and individuals. Should they find information on one listing site (e.g., Yelp, Abaco, CitySearch, Merchants Circle, Manta, YP.com, BBB, and more than 300 more), they pick it up and push it to the others. Guess what? Just because the information is correct today doesn't mean it will be correct a month from now.

And are you aware that anyone can claim your listing and publish whatever information they choose? That's a simple way to destroy a firm's online rankings. Some sites are not only listings but review sites as well. It's a full-time job to keep all these listings straight. Some services manage that for you.

Review Sites – Sites such as Yahoo, Facebook, Yelp, TripAdvisor, Amazon, Foursquare, Bing, Google, and many others have specific rules and regulations for posting product or service reviews. It's easy to have a review posted online, but it's often difficult to remove it if it is less than flattering. So you need to devise a monitoring process where someone monitors your social sites and reviews them on a routine basis, even daily. A lot can happen to a business with a 1-star review and no commentary from the business owner.

As for your professional environment, prospective and existing clients get to see where the magic happens: your offices. Are you a solopreneur? Multiple partners? Medium-sized firm with a lot of asset managers? Multiple offices and staffing to handle large accounts?

Employees and Contemporaries – Those who work for and with you are equally important. You rely on them for open, friendly, yet formal communications. After all, you're dealing with people's money. You and your team hold the future of your client's and their families' lives. There can't be any laissez-faire attitude or actions. People are counting on you to be as serious as they were when they handed you their wealth. They depend on you for their future.

It's important to keep your staff informed of all they need to know in order to properly serve your clients and the assets they brought with them. Treating people with respect and understanding doesn't end with the client. Your fellow wealth managers, financial advisors, or whatever moniker you use deserve that same respect and trust.

Your Professional Brand – Do your grooming and attire reflect a successful individual? What about your staff? Do they reflect a professional image that would instill confidence if someone walked in the door at any moment? What about the furniture, fixtures, and equipment in your offices? Is it fresh and new, well maintained?

Are your computers up-to-date, or are they in need of an upgrade? What about hand-held devices and the software to power them? And what about those plants? Are they fresh or plastic? How about refreshments? Snacks? In other words, what is a client's or prospect's first impression?

Internal "Magnetic" Marketing – Magnetic Marketing is a term Dan Kennedy coined to describe data-driven internal marketing. And "magnetic" is what we like to call marketing. It is the key to unlocking our entire world, and it can unlock yours. We learned this at the 10,000-hour university—reading, listening, attending, living, and breathing everything Dan Kennedy had to offer. I'm so confident in Dan's teachings that I became one of his clients. He was my mentor, coach, confidant, and friend until he became terminally ill and ended all his professional engagements. But enough about me. I need to discuss internal marketing.

In your business, there are multiple markets you can see. There are employees, and there are clients—active and inactive. All these internal market segments require attention.

They are in your view; they are what you can see. You can see the ongoing relationship with your clients and their families. You can see the relationship with your own family as you do your best to support them. You can see your employees who cheeringly provide friendly support as they see you succeed. You can see your fellow contemporaries at your side, ensuring the best possible outcomes for your clients and their families. Their financial futures are in the same hands that hold your own future.

There are many things in sight on the surface of the water where your ship—your business—floats. I hope what I've shared with you will open your eyes and remove your rose-colored glasses about life on the high seas. Those seas are your everyday life in the business, the career, you have chosen.

Your family is counting on you just as much as your clients are to be successful. Your family's and your clients' lives and futures are in your hands.

In the next chapter, we'll reveal what lies beneath the surface of the water—the not-so-visible parts of the iceberg that can sink you.

The Middle of The Funnel (MOFU)

Identifying Your External Market

*Keep yourself positive, cheerful and goal-oriented. Sales
success is 80% attitude and only 20% aptitude.*

—Brian Tracy

IN THIS CHAPTER, we'll explore what's under the surface of
the water—that part of your business marketplace you don't always
notice. If your business iceberg is like thousands of other small business icebergs, there are a great many marketing opportunities that
elude you. A lot goes on below the surface that may never even
come to your attention. And you may not see the invisible glacier
below that appears to be a manageable obstacle or challenge but can
produce catastrophic harm to the "ship" you call your business.

To a certain extent, your business is like all businesses. Every business suffers setbacks from time to time. They have difficulties with staff, vendors, a poor economy, the market, competition. All these and more are the common and routine challenges to which all businesses are susceptible. However, each business also faces a multitude of concerns and troubles. There's a lot to do when operating a business and a lot of decisions to make on the spur of the moment.

EXTERNAL MARKETING

You probably don't see all the results of your external marketing efforts. A business with some know-how utilizes different phone numbers for each external marketing asset. There are numbers to call for each print ad that is distributed—newspaper, magazine, flyer, brochure. The different phone numbers tell you where the lead originated. Why is that important?

It's important because you will learn over time which assets are producing leads and which ones are not performing as well. Heck, some might not be producing anything. Knowing this valuable data can tell you where to divert your marketing budget. Without hard data like that, you're floating blind.

What you don't see are the inquiries, the interviews, the e-mails, the texts, the discussions at networking events, and so on *because you don't track them*. You probably don't see each transactional inflow of assets to manage. You probably only see them as one total number.

BELIEVE IN YOURSELF

Doubting yourself is often the beginning of the end. That is why it is so important to seek constant learning on all aspects of your profession. Direct response marketing is also important. In fact, it's the difference between doing well and doing fantastic. Digest direct marketing books, CDs, videos, conferences, and workshops at every opportunity. Expand your professional brand and grow your client base as large as you can handle.

As you work toward growing your spheres of influence, be sure to build solid relationships. Often the question is this: "Who do you know?" But the real questions should be this: "Who knows you and how do they feel about you?" And let's go even further: "How many people like, trust, and respect you?"

So far, you've seen a lot of what is (or should be) visible on the surface of your business "ocean." We've looked in detail at all the things you must pay attention to in order to ensure your firm is functioning the way you originally intended when you first hung up your shingle. There is quite a bit more that you may not notice so easily.

I realize that nearly all of you reading this book didn't receive any marketing training before you entered this self-employment situation you find yourself in. Most professional services firms are in the same boat. When you were studying, learning, apprenticing, and cutting your teeth in this fine vocation, chances are you didn't learn how to market your practice once you were on your own. It's a pity, but it is the truth.

It was the same for me when I came to this country from India. My wife, my son, and I came to the United States for a better life. I am educated, knowledgeable, and proficient as a data scientist. I've experienced success and failure on multiple occasions. However, when I met Bill Glazer and Dan Kennedy, my entire life changed.

Hopefully, you're grasping all aspects of what makes a successful financial advisor business. But there's more. Let's look next at what else is below the surface of your business—more of the so-called iceberg under the ocean.

DATA SCIENCE

Are you tracking each visitor who stops by your website, hangs around, and then leaves without clicking on your calls to action? Do you know there is software that can tell you who visited your site, even if they were there for only a few seconds? That's data you don't see because it's so hidden, so far beneath the surface.

Maintaining and analyzing data are the keys to maximizing revenues through a complex audit of the past. <u>You don't see the missed opportunities</u>. You don't see the frequency of asset ebb and flow for each prospect or client. You don't see patterns of behavior through numbers. It takes expertise to spot past trends, patterns, anomalies, and mistakes. *The untrained eye misses all this valuable information.*

There happens to be an entire world of data science and data brokerage you don't see. You're probably not a data geek like I am. There is a whole world all its own that is extremely sophisticated and complex. It takes years to learn how to unlock the gems that are buried in your data files. You don't see the data because you have little or no education in data science. If you understand a little, you can learn a great deal. I take my clients through the mining of data so they grasp the importance of what I do.

At eLaunchers, we start our journey by developing a **1,000-day roadmap** divided into the following parts:

- **Planning:** 1 to 12 days
- **Building systems:** 13 to 100 days

◆ **Launch and get results:** 101 to 300 days
◆ **Get return on investments:** 301 to 1,000 days and beyond

We're going to discuss all these audit sequences to "find money" and sharpen your ideal client avatar. But hang on for a while. We'll get to it.

Most people are completely unaware of the benefit of data, let alone how to dig for the hidden treasures in that data. Let me give you a complete workbook I wrote on this. It's called ***Magnetic Marketing Implementation A.B.C.D. Any Business Can Do***. E-mail me at pshah@eLaunchers.com, and I'll make sure you get a copy. We'll look at performing this type of analysis a little later in the book.

FLOATING HUMANS

People float in and out of your life every day. You meet them on the street, at the grocery store, at the library. There are people everywhere. Each time you meet someone at a networking event, you might exchange business cards. Will you ever hear from them? Will they ever hear from you? I know of many business owners who make what seems to be a hobby of accepting business cards, adding them to a stack on their desk or in a drawer, or maybe tossing them in a trash can. They have no real intention to follow up. Sure, they may have had a weak, flimsy, conscious plan to follow up. But when reality and life settle in, they'll probably never find the time to call the number on that business card.

The people you meet casually and then forget aren't family. They're not even friends. They're just someone at an event, at the store, or at the library making small talk. But one day, they might become your client. One of their family members or relatives might one day be your client. They might even be a real estate investor with millions in assets. What's your next move?

SORTING HUMANS

List segmentation is one of my favorite topics because it is specifically about data. I love data. I love the mathematical and scientific modeling of data. But I digress so let me get to sorting.

Not seeing or realizing the importance of your ideal prospects and their individual characteristics is another area where many people fall flat. Prospects are not just faceless, ageless, genderless prospects; they are unique human beings. By segmenting your prospect or lead lists, you can communicate better with them. Perhaps you already separate them by wealth tiers. Perhaps you segment them by gender, by age, or even by type of asset portfolio. However, if you try to see below the surface—your prospect list—you can see a much more complex gathering of individuals.

DEEP SEGMENTATION

List segmentation is an extremely efficient way to keep track of your prospects. There are ways to do that, and one of them is lead scoring. Even lead scoring comes in different versions, depending on how the data user received training. There are also sophisticated software platforms that utilize thousands of data touchpoints from information on the entire Internet. In addition to basic demographics, the software scours the Web for patterns in dozens and even hundreds of areas.

Behavioral nuances, buying patterns, selling patterns, even negative markers can be identified. Once they are collected, the program spits out a predicted model on that individual, forecasting the likelihood of him or her becoming a client. Manual lead scoring is practically useless compared to machine learning, artificial intelligence (AI), and real data science.

The same thing applies to your existing and former clients. A tweak here, a tweak there can yield a literal boatload of data to be harvested and studied. The predictive analytics software systems can spot irregularities and patterns, both positive and negative. With all of this data at your fingertips, you can rule the world—at least your future world.

Seeing this data while working your already busy day is unlikely. Without the expertise to translate the data into actionable information, you won't benefit from any of it. That's the value my company brings daily to financial advisors, wealth managers, and services providers. As one of the few, true data scientists in the field of direct response marketing, I'm confident with what I share with my clients.

LIST RENTING AND PURCHASING

There are very specific ways to get a list for a direct mail campaign. The average person might ask the list broker for a list of a specific area that includes demographic information and matches their ideal prospect. That's all well and good. It's typical.

For example, my co-author, Rodger Friedman, shared with me that early in his direct mail education, he rented a list of names based on income, home ownership, zip code, and political party affiliation. His mailing fell flat on its face because he knew practically nothing about his list other than where they lived and how they vote. That my friends, is skinny data!

But an informed list buyer knows what to ask for and what to leave out. They don't want duplicates, erroneous addresses, old lists, retail addresses mixed with residential, and vice versa. Those and more are some of the things you want to leave out of any list you intend to transact.

However, there are things you should be sure to include on the list. They are much more important than the geographic area, the correct addresses (although that's important, too), and names. There are all sorts of markers that help segment a population by behavior, industry, business title, buying habits, frequency of name on other lists, and so on and so on. You should try to identify 10 to 15 markers in order to fully segment the list you request. You should also ask for a written guarantee that the list will be fresh and the information valid. And be sure to request a credit for each undeliverable piece of mail.

So now you've got a pretty good education on list segmentation for prospects and clients. And what hasn't been visible is suddenly becoming visible! You are more informed about what's under the surface—that bigger part of the iceberg.

Challenges are what make life interesting and overcoming them is what makes life meaningful.

—Joshua J. Marine

THE MARKETING CYCLE

Regardless of industry, sector, subsector, or niche market, the marketing cycle is the same for everyone. The *Deming Cycle, a continuous improvement model,* was the foundation for the Four Phases of a Marketing Cycle. Here are those phases:

1. Measurement and Analysis
2. Strategic Planning
3. Implementation
4. Market Response

From the initial conversation with a prospect, my data science brain kicks into high gear, all the way to signing account documents and funding the accounts. You will benefit from adopting this four-phase line of thinking when it comes to client acquisition and nurturing.

The Marketing Cycle is a rinse-and-repeat process to ensure you monitor and adjust as much as you can when it becomes evident that something is out of whack. Think of the process as a wheel in constant motion. Let's look at these four phases.

1. Measurement and Analysis: Strategic business plans are one thing, but opportunist marketing is quite another for generating business growth. Data is what must be analyzed, and KPIs (key performance indicators) must be measured and metrics verified.

When I have a client who decides to take on eLaunchers for our service offerings, I perform an integrated analysis of the past three years of data, both financial and operational. Knowledge is power, and the ability to understand what the data is saying is critical to all future steps. Revenue forecasting data becomes available based on established goals and objectives.

2. Strategic Planning: Scope, resources, goals, and action steps are the elements of a powerful marketing plan. Spending time to thoroughly digest the wants, desires, needs, and problems requires deep thought based on all the information gathered.

The strategic planning portion of the marketing cycle is perhaps the most important part of the cycle. Not having a clear action plan based on sound information can make or break a campaign or a business. Understanding revenue forecasting and monetizing every step of the plan are extremely important.

This plan is responsible for available data, goals, objectives, strategic action, and assigned metrics. It is also responsible for awareness building, communicating the message to market match, choosing the channels to distribute the messaging for the greatest acceptance and receipt, monetizing the offering, and predicting revenue outcomes based on all data available.

3. **Implementation:** Executing the strategic plan addresses all the details in the entire campaign effort. The measurement and analysis team thoroughly considers the strategic plan and completely verifies it. Then, on-the-fly, decision-making is possible, and that's when the unexpected occurs. No matter how much time and effort are dedicated to measurement, analysis, planning, and implementation, it is never perfect. Fully knowledgeable decision-makers can save the day.

4. **Marketing Response:** The market's acceptance of the offering is in the hands of the consumer, not the firm. Proficient, initial steps have been taken to get to this point, and at that point, whether the consumer accepts or declines the offer is out of the seller's hands. Using direct response magnetic marketing elevates the acceptance of the offer's value proposition.

eLaunchers' clients follow what we call the "One System." Just like we do, they utilize several "props" to assist in the marketing cycle. We recommend *giving* before ever *asking* for anything. It might be a shock-and-awe portfolio, a Wow Box, or a variety of educational materials such as books. They are completely unexpected and quickly increase trust. Nurture sequences continue to build trust and familiarity until the desired outcome is reached. It's my philosophy that if I make friends first, I'll make money later.

23

The Bottom of the Funnel (BOFU)

. . . . . .

When They are Ready to Buy

Some people are at the top of the ladder, some are in the middle, still more are at the bottom, and a whole lot more don't even know there is a ladder.

—Robert H. Schuller

BY THE TIME our prospect arrives near the bottom of the funnel, many things are happening. The prospect might receive additional gifts and nurture pieces, perhaps an estimate, perhaps a case presentation system, and any information that is still required to eliminate all doubt.

POST-CLOSE OPPORTUNITIES

Congratulations may be in order. If you've successfully taken a prospect through your funnel system, you have made a friend and increased your Assets under Management (AUM).

At eLaunchers, our post-close process is what we refer to as **orientation and onboarding**. It's a formalized process and system to ensure everything is documented, comprehensive, and agreed to by all parties.

ASCENSION

Ascension is a post-close process that is ongoing for the length of the client's relationship with you. *By ascension, we mean elevating or increasing overall revenues from each client.*

What can you do to grow additional AUM? There are several opportunities for that with a structured ascension plan.

Ask yourself what, if any, funds or assets are currently not under your care. Is the current AUM just a portion of your client's assets? What can you do to get additional assets to bolster your client's account under your care? And in addition to AUM, what about insurance reviews, other types of insurance, and long-term care?

And be sure to inquire about family members who are not under your care. What is the likelihood of converting these family members so they will relocate their existing assets and retirement plans to your care and maintenance?

RETENTION

The primary objective is to *control the client's AUM for as long as possible*—years from the time of acquisition. You do that by establishing fail-safe communications that are completely automated yet personal. Except for market failure, there should be no reason for a client to leave and go to someone else.

Your objective should also be to continue to care for a client's assets when they are no longer with us. If there happens to be a death or a break-up of the family for any reason, your responsibility is to remain a trusted advisor and stay with the AUM.

Occasionally, something may cause a departure or restructuring of the AUM. By remaining the care provider for the client's assets, you can be the consistency and security the family needs when there's a windfall income or fiscal distress.

Be sure to provide **ongoing education** for the members of the client's family regarding the outcome of the income and the value of managing a client's fiscal affairs through all life events.

Client lifetime value (CLV) is extremely important, and it happens when you maintain and elevate your relationship with the client.

ADVOCACY

Creating raving fans—or what we refer to as **advocacy**—can often make a modest effort elevate your AUM to heights not yet experienced. I mentioned earlier in the book about providing consistent communication, unexpected extras, and highly personalized correspondence that can usually turn long-term clients into your secret sales force. You need an active system of encouraging referrals. They come through your clients whose loyalty, trust, and friendliness are at their peak because of all your efforts.

Through gentle, unobtrusive coaching and encouragement, you can <u>identify ideal referrals</u>, and your client base can grow exponentially.

Through expressions of gratitude without attempting to bribe them into helping you, referrals can populate without much effort or expense.

Remember the principle: **<u>Referrals are EARNED, not BOUGHT!</u>**

I certainly hope the information I have shared with you is valuable, useful, and implementable.

Rodger and I truly appreciate the investment you have made in this book and the time you have spent absorbing its contents to secure the kind of future we know you can experience.

There's one more very valuable chapter. In the next and final chapter, we'll give you short explanations of the product and service offerings we utilize to grow businesses exponentially.

PART III

eLaunchers
Marketing Services

SOLUTIONS FOR EFFECTIVE MARKETING

elaunchers' Tools for Effective Marketing

. . . .

Product and Service Offerings

*Twenty years from now, you will be more disappointed by
the things you didn't do than the ones you did do. So throw
off the bowlines. Sail away from the safe harbor. Catch
the winds in your sails. Explore. Dream. Discover.*

—Mark Twain

THIS CHAPTER CONTAINS some specific product offerings you may find helpful and interesting. They are the product and service offerings eLaunchers routinely uses to assist our clients in growing their conversion.

**Ultimate Conversion Concepts Platform
The PERFECT TOOL to keep prospects
who have not said YES yet.**

**The PERFECT TOOL to engage clients
in the decision-making process.
The PERFECT TOOL if clients are moving
down the buying continuum.**

Snapshot: The Ultimate Conversion Concepts Platform (UCCP) contains multiple copy assets. Each one is designed to answer questions, handle objections, provide logical and emotional reasons to buy, keep prospects engaged, and move them closer to making a purchase decision.

Discussion: Every business has a funnel:

1. **Lead generation** happens at the TOP of the funnel.
2. Based on the information you provide, the MIDDLE of the funnel is where prospects decide to *BUY, NOT BUY, or NOT BUY NOW.*
3. A prospect becomes a customer or client at the BOTTOM of the funnel when they are ready to have a **serious conversation.**

Most businesses have a process to generate TOP OF THE FUNNEL leads. And most are good at the BOTTOM OF THE FUNNEL—closing a sale with a willing buyer.

However, most new leads do not buy on first contact. So what does that mean? Without a process to stay in touch with prospects who don't buy immediately and move them to a BOTTOM OF THE FUNNEL **buying conversation,** the MAJORITY of your leads are wasted and do you no good whatsoever. And generating those lost leads **cost you money.**

How do you move prospects from the TOP OF THE FUNNEL to the MIDDLE OF THE FUNNEL?

By staying in touch and providing them with information. That's where you **educate** prospects and build their interest. Then you can **move them FROM the fact-finding MIDDLE TO the buying-conversation BOTTOM of the funnel.** The purpose of UCCP is to give you **MAXIMUM RETURN on every dollar you invest in lead generation.**

UCCP INCLUDES an entire marketing process, including assets for lead generation. It also has a unique variety of powerful copy assets to educate middle-of-the-funnel prospects, build their interest, and move them toward a buying decision.

UCCP assets such as Shock & Awe, Case Presentation, Chair Side Marketing, Referral Culture, and more **tell your story, answer questions, present your case, handle objections, and get people to realize your product or service is right for them.**

The Ultimate Conversion Concepts Platform is the PERFECT TOOL to:

- Keep prospects ENGAGED
- Move them through the MIDDLE OF THE FUNNEL
- Stimulate BUYING CONVERSATIONS
- Give you MAXIMUM VALUE on every dollar you invest in lead generation

UCCP is ideal for any business owner or professional who does not have a **proven process** to keep prospects interested and moving toward a buying decision.

The Problems UCCP Solves:

1. Gives you a **PROVEN PROCESS** to keep prospects engaged and moving toward a buying decision.
2. Gives you a **SYSTEMATIC WAY** to educate prospects, so when they are ready, they will contact you essentially pre-sold and ready to buy.
3. Gives you a **DEPENDABLE STRATEGY to REALIZE MAXIMUM BENEFIT** from every dollar you invest in lead generation.
4. Gives you **POWERFUL SALES TOOLS** ideal for a variety of situations.
5. Gives you a **LONG-TERM SOLUTION** you pay for once and may benefit from for years to come—to move prospects through the middle of the funnel and generate sales continuously.

eLaunchers' UCCP program is one of the most successful services we offer. The Ultimate Conversion Concepts Program leads the ideal prospect from the top of the funnel (TOFU), through the middle of the funnel (MOFU), and all the way to the bottom of the funnel (BOFU). UCCP is a combination of ongoing educational nurturing and engagement. It provides positive lead flow through the entire buyer's journey (continuum) to conversion for many years to come because it is based on PROVEN MARKETING AND SALES PRINCIPLES.

Another program eLaunchers offers is our Private-Client Services Program. Like any high-performing team effort, your marketing implementation will sail more smoothly with ongoing care and maintenance of your vessel. Ongoing monitoring of what works and what doesn't in a live setting is a critical element and a sophisticated system that produces accelerated growth.

eLaunchers' Private Client Monthly Services

The PERFECT SOLUTION for the BUSINESS OWNER or PROFESSIONAL who wants EFFECTIVE MARKETING TO RUN SEAMLESSLY IN THE BACKGROUND

The PERFECT SOLUTION for the BUSINESS OWNER or PROFESSIONAL who wants MAXIMUM RETURN on every dollar invested to build their business

ELAUNCHERS' MONTHLY SERVICES CLIENTS

Snapshot: Do you need help with your business-growth strategy? What about your problem-solving and marketing campaign design and implementation? Or list research, graphic design, offer creation, and funnel building? eLaunchers' Monthly Services Clients have **the full power of one of the most highly regarded digital marketing agencies in America** to work seamlessly in the background to generate leads for you. We educate your prospects, keep them engaged, make sales, and build your business.

Discussion: eLaunchers' Private Monthly Service Clients all share this in common: They want effective marketing that delivers a **continuous stream of good prospects**, requires very little of their time or their employees' time, and runs seamlessly in the background.

Private Clients tend to stay for years. *Why?* Because **eLaunchers gets things done.** We make your life easier. We keep prospects engaged. We make the cash register ring. We administer your entire pixel estate. From your website and social media to your blog, sales funnels, quarterly marketing campaigns, and more—we handle it all for you, leaving you free to serve customers or clients and manage other parts of your business.

Private Client Monthly Services are FULLY CUSTOMIZED to meet your needs.

Monthly services may include blog distribution, quarterly marketing campaigns, e-mail marketing, direct mail, graphic design, weekly sales meetings with your team, newsletter set-up and distribution, printing and mailing, strategy meetings, monthly CEO debriefings, and more.

Everything happens seamlessly in the background. We handle it all.

You would need several highly skilled, full-time employees to deliver the services you receive as a member of the eLaunchers Private Client Monthly Service Group.

The moment you become a Private Monthly Services Client, the entire eLaunchers organization of skilled marketing professionals is on your team. Think of it as an elite, outsourced marketing department that generates leads, educates prospects, nurtures them until they are ready to buy, drives sales, and produces results directly attributable to our efforts. We take the burden of depending on in-house personnel to generate leads, nurture prospects, drive sales, and manage digital assets.

The eLaunchers' Private Monthly Services Client offering is ideal for any eLaunchers' UCCP marketing package client. It's ideal for any business owner who depends on good leads to build their business. It's for any business owner *who acknowledges that having an entire team of professionals with a long history of delivering excellent results working together to build your business* is preferable to trying to wing it with employees with no special marketing training and no documented history of business-building performance.

The Problems This Solves:

◆ Brings **full accountability** to your marketing.
◆ Delivers a **measurable ROI** directly attributable to each marketing activity.
◆ Gives you a 1,000-day **STRATEGIC PLAN** to build your business and reach important goals, complete with timelines for accomplishment, and an entire team of marketing professionals working on your behalf.

One of the short-term decisions some clients contemplate is believing they can function on their own without a professional automation and creation team involved. Some of our former clients have made that decision. Several of these fine humans have managed to keep the ship afloat and have headed in the right direction. Occasionally, I receive a call from a client asking advice on an issue, which I am happy to give. Good for them. We must have taught them well.

My friends can always have my time. We continue to wish them great success.

But there is another segment of this same group that doesn't fare quite as well. It's unfortunate for them, and I take it personally because I must not have imparted enough knowledge for them to stay the course. But some of them have called for help; they've come upon an iceberg of sorts. The eLaunchers team spring-loads into action and gets right into the mix to course-correct and bring that business back on course.

Our ongoing care and maintenance monthly services program helps our clients avoid the rough seas and any pending disasters.

Success Blueprint

THE SUCCESS BLUEPRINT is the steps to follow for a successful outcome. eLaunchers does this without fail for every new client.

STEPS 1–4: FIRST 12 DAYS – ORIENTATION AND ONBOARDING

Step 1 – Step one is the Magnetic Marketing System Implementation A.B.C.D. (Any Business Can Do) Workbook. You can download it, or we can mail one to you along with a toolbox. Complete this entire workbook to the best of your ability. I, Parthiv Shah, will personally go over this with you. Together we'll figure out who you are, who you are for, and why your customers should do business with you.

Step 2 – Step two is to schedule a call with me by going to https://elaunchers.com/client/ to access my appointment calendar. Pick a day and time that works best for you. Make sure to be on time since we will have a lot of information to go over and verify. I'll verify and dig a bit deeper into the questions you've already answered and discuss any you have not answered. I'll go over a 73-point revenue checklist to identify all the ways you are generating revenue and some other ways we can consider including in your marketing plan.

Step 3 – Step three is one of the most important exercises we'll conduct. It's what I like to call *the Everest Planning Session*. It's where we establish how we will ascend to the summit from the bottom of the mountain. We'll map out a three- to five-year trip, beginning with the end in mind. As Dr. Stephen Covey said, the only way to get where you are going is to identify your ultimate destination.

So with the end in mind, we set out our course to ascend securely, campsites along the way, and follow a timeline. Consider eLaunchers your Sherpa. The Sherpa is a guide who knows the trails for maximum ascent and knows what pitfalls to avoid. Hiking, carrying the gear, and doing part of the work along the way are the responsibility of the hiker. I cannot carry the entire load. We climb together.

We'll utilize a pair of systems provided by DigitalMarketer (eLaunchers is a Certified Partner). The co-founder, Ryan Deiss, is a personal friend and colleague. We often refer clients to each other. One system is the Ultimate Value Journey Canvas, and the other is the Ultimate Customer Value Optimization plan. We'll work on them together to maximize value equations and strategies for your business. From the information we uncover, we'll create a <u>two-page marketing plan</u>.

Step 4 – Step four of the Success Blueprint is the meat and potatoes. It's Data Intelligence and Administration. This step is my favorite because it's when I determine all the data points that culminate into a metric. And I create a lot of metrics. The purpose of analysis and measurement is to **identify what is working and what is not**, what needs tweaking and what is completely useless and needs replacement. It also clearly tells us where we're getting the highest return on investment by where leads originate.

We'll establish control reviews for Google and Facebook ad reports, heatmaps, budget reviews, ROI reports, and a litany of other data deliverables. Every time I do this, it's like playing with new toys.

We accomplish all this and much more within the first 12 days of your coming onboard. You will also be required to assemble a portfolio of every marketing asset you have ever created, used, copied, or swiped and deployed. I'll perform an audit on the previous 1,000 days of financial activity to spot anomalies, spikes, dips, and irregularities and see how and from whom cash flow rolls in. This audit can find what I like to call **"Diamonds in Your Database."** There is also a proprietary process I use to find lost opportunities, missed opportunities, and opportunities for regeneration of former customers.

STEPS 5–8: DAYS 13–100 – ORGANIZATION AND DEVELOPMENT OF DELIVERABLES

Step 5 – In step five, we **establish the Four Estates, the Four Ps—the Pixel Estate**. This estate is where all your digital assets live. Included are your blogs, web pages, search engine optimization, calls-to-action, social media, landing pages, e-mails, CRM, and analytics. We'll determine what level of upgrading or downgrading each pixel tool requires as we work through the individual assignments.

Step 6 – Step six is called **the Paper Estate**. Earlier, I referred to my Shock & Awe package, my Wow Box, and all they contain. We're going to identify and develop a creative plan for every marketing asset you will use in print. Mind you, some of these will be dual-purpose: digital and printed.

Just about every practitioner (attorneys, physicians, dentists, chiropractors, opticians, financial planners, wealth managers, CPAs, and more) uses or should use a Case Presentation Packet. We'll create one of them for **YOU**, along with special reports, checklists, e-books, white papers, and everything imaginable to put you in the best light.

One more thing we'll plan and create is a formal Referral Marketing System (part of your Internal Marketing). Referral Marketing is an important strategic set of tools that brings in your best customers. They're preconditioned to like and trust you based on the recommendation and referral from their family member or friend.

Step 7 – Step seven is **the People Estate**—identifying and onboarding all the humans involved with your project for the next 100 days at a minimum. Beyond that, it will depend on how many and what type of marketing assets you request or we recommend. Some might need copywriting, while others might need only graphics, and so on.

Included in this People Estate are a Web Team, Graphics Team, Data Team, System Engineering Team, Telephone Marketing Team, Marketing Technology Management Team, Copy Team, Content Team, QA & Proof Team, Traffic Team, and Production Team.

Step 8 – Step eight is **the Place Estate**. We'll review your physical place of business—everything from the city, town, or community you live and work in to your actual office space. You'll describe in detail the street address(es), the floor (if multi-story), the suite number, and so on. We'll discuss your office layout, reception area, meeting rooms, and layout of the entire space, including any inventory and storage rooms, other facilities, and the like. Where do you store your documents and files? Is there a break room or lunch room? What about recreation areas? Guest refreshment bar? Staff refreshment bar? We will document theses descriptions and keep them in your file.

What about wall hangings, art, desk, and table accoutrements? We'll have you describe the total ambiance of each area of your office suite, especially where your office and meeting areas for prospect meetings are located.

STEPS 9–12: DAYS 101–1,000 – THE MARKETING MIX

Step 9 – Step nine is the **Ultimate Web Traffic Platform**, or establishing online traffic sources and processes. These are both organically earned. They include paid web traffic, social media traffic, referral sites, affiliate or reseller relations, offline to online traffic, offline traffic from direct mail, television, and radio.

We're at the point in this step where all the marketing communications assets have been repurposed from the portfolio of past marketing assets. We're also where all the new marketing assets created over the past 100 days are put to work to generate traffic, lead identification, lead nurturing, client and prospect education, affiliate education, and new systems processes. Together with everything else, this makes brand growth and revenue growth a reality.

Step 10 – This step is **Ultimate Conversion Concepts**. It's the processes and systems that cause and manage lead capture, lead follow-up, nurture campaigns, pre-appointment engagements, and communications for no-shows and no-sales. They also include new client welcome sequences, surveys, feedback requests, and ongoing e-mail sequences for digital info-share (weekly mini-news).

Step 11 – This step is called **Ultimate Phone Follow-Up**. Regardless of how the prospect or lead was acquired, e-mail and texting are NOT acceptable. Phone follow-up is what you must do in order to evaluate, qualify, and convert prospects so they take the next step. It might be to request more information or a demo. It could be to have a discussion or ask questions on pricing, features, and benefits. You're not able to provide a Q&A source that's comprehensive enough to satisfy every query.

This step involves tracking every attempt and every prospect action (downloaded report, opened an e-mail, tracked lead marketing sources such as websites, referrals, news media, social media, webinars, etc.). Each channel should have a phone number to track inbound inquiries and understand what is working and which works best. If a channel doesn't perform as well as others, tweak it until it does.

At eLaunchers, we have **a fail-safe phone follow-up system**. It is essentially like this: Follow-up calls will continue with regularity until the prospect either signs or unsubscribes, opts out, tells us off, or worse. Then and only then do we cease communications. Why? Because they raised their hand to learn more. But maybe they're not ready to buy now. What about next week, next month, next year?

Step 12 – In this final step, **Training and Documentation**, every note, communications note, mind map, e-mail, transcription, or marketing asset goes into a binder specifically dedicated to that specific clien. They include but are not limited to training materials and session recaps, marketing manuals, training videos, spreadsheets, and workbooks. If it has to do with communicating with the client in any manner, it goes into the binder. That binder might morph into multiple binders, and that's fine. The more documentation the better if you want to replace a key player.

As we move along the timeline, you and I—your coach and guide—will move along a progressive path toward the outcomes and goals we established at the onset of our relationship. Remember the Everest Plan? We're making our way to the summit.

The Success Blueprint is a great way to analyze your existing business model, goals, and objectives, as well as your strengths and weaknesses.

Done For You

· · · · · · ·

High-Value Client Marketing Machine

Think of prospects who are IDEAL for your HIGH-VALUE PRODUCT or SERVICE.

Do you want them to contact you after they're WELL-INFORMED *and* WANTING TO KNOW MORE?

This may be the *PERFECT TOOL* for you.

ANOTHER ELAUNCHERS PRODUCT offering is our HVC—a Done-for-You Marketing Machine. This service offering is specifically designed to generate leads and conversion using a direct response mail campaign. This program targets the most well-defined, *ideal prospects* for your product or service from the top 5% of the wealthy in the country or your local area.

If you have a product or service that is geared to the top financially wealthy in the population, that system is IDEAL, the **PERFECT TOOL**.

Snapshot: The **HIGH-VALUE CLIENT PROGRAM** is a multi-step, **done-for-you** marketing campaign designed to (1) initiate interest in new prospects or (2) reengage unconverted prospects in your database who would ideally benefit from your premium product or service.

HVC includes (1) deep-dive list research to identify prospects for your premium product or service (list research by list expert Parthiv Shah); (2) four custom direct-response letters written to GET A RESPONSE and other marketing assets written by master sales letter copywriter Russell Martino, and (3) all graphics, printing, FedEx, and direct-mail delivery.

The High-Value Client Marketing Machine is the PERFECT TOOL to:

IDENTIFY AND CONNECT WITH YOUR HIGHEST VALUE, TOP 5% OF THE PYRAMID, MOST AFFLUENT PROSPECTS—AND GET A RESPONSE.

Purpose: Generate inbound interest from highly qualified prospects. Get new or existing prospects for your premium product or service to contact you, ready to learn more.

Ideal for: Any business or professional who wants high-quality leads—leads who know who you are and know what you do—to contact you (or your designee) because they want to learn more.

What HVC Campaigns Accomplish for You: (1) IDENTIFY and CONNECT WITH high-value prospects who are a good match for your premium product or service and (2) REKINDLE INTEREST in unconverted leads and get them to contact you.

Who this will benefit: This will help any business owner or professional with a HIGH DOLLAR PRODUCT OR SERVICE or a HIGH LIFETIME VALUE OF A CUSTOMER OR CLIENT who wants to reach people well-suited for their premium offer. It benefits anyone who *wants those prospects to contact them when they are interested, well-informed, and ready to learn more.*

Applications:

1. **Revive Unconverted Leads**: HVC Campaigns help you connect with and GET A RESPONSE from **unconverted leads** who may otherwise sit idle, instead of contacting you when they're excited to learn more.
2. **Excellent Source of New Leads:** HVC includes laser-targeted list research that will identify 1,000 or more prospects for your premium product or service.
3. **An Excellent Tool to:** (1) bypass e-mail, adwords, search, social media, and the Internet altogether and (2) get a series of engaging letters and other marketing assets in the hands of HIGHLY QUALIFIED PROSPECTS by FedEx and direct mail.

Problems HVC Solves: (1) There are no more iffy leads. HVC identifies highly qualified prospects for your premium product or service; (2) FedEx and direct mail have a near 100% deliver and open rate, so your high-value prospects WILL receive your messages; (3) with copy by master copywriter Russell Martino, you have a STRONG MESSAGE-TO-MARKET MATCH that will capture and hold attention, giving your messages a high probability of getting a fast response.

Our High-Value Client solution is one of the lead generation campaign offerings we are most proud of. The benefit our clients receive from this service is a direct response campaign written by our master copywriter, Russell Martino. HVC is designed to reach the top 5% of wealth prospects in a manner that is unheard of in most circles. The platform benefits the client because this campaign is also duplicable; you can use it again and again.

The list research is so finely tuned that after targeted ideal prospects are contacted, there is a nearly 100% delivery and open rate. The message-to-market match captures and holds the attention of the reader, producing a high level of a quick request for more information.

Within these offerings, only the most productive, attractive, and magnetic copywriting will do. eLaunchers' Master Copywriter Russell Martino of Conquest Marketing is one of the highest in demand and the highest paid in the country. Russell's expertise is founded on the principles of his direct response marketing expertise. His level of the deep psychological triggers required in copy is his greatest asset. On the next page is a letter that will tell more about him.

eLaunchers' Smart Start New Lead Development Program

A Powerful Solution to Identify and Connect with Prospects Ideal for Your Premium Product or Service

A Way to Avoid the Inefficiency Expense and Hassle of On-line Lead Development

SNAPSHOT: The eLaunchers Smart Start New Lead Development Program includes the following:

- **Expert list research** to identify at least 2,500 laser-targeted prospects who are ideal to benefit from your products or services.
- Two professionally written **two-page letters** to generate interest and solicit a response for more information.
- One professionally written follow-up, large format **postcard**.
- All **graphics, printing, and mailing costs**, including postage, to 2,500 laser-targeted prospects.

Purpose: New lead development is the purpose of the Smart

Start New Lead Development Program. It is designed to find, connect with, and get a response from high-quality new leads who may be perfect to benefit from your products or services. It can eliminate the problems, inefficiency, expense, and hassle of online lead prospecting.

Ideal for: The program is for any business or professional who (1) wants responsive, high-quality leads who know what you do and request more information and (2) wants to minimize marketing costs by weeding out tire-kickers and unqualified leads before launching a multi-step direct marketing campaign that may include FedEx and direct mail.

What eLaunchers Smart Start Program accomplishes for you: Smart Start gives you a fully-vetted list of at least 2,500 prospects who are ideal to benefit from what you sell. It provides full, out-the-door implementation, including copywriting, graphics, printing, and mailing.

People who respond to the Smart Start campaign and request more information are serious prospects. And that justifies the expense of extensive follow-up, which may include multiple sales letters, a Shock & Awe box, and other marketing assets.

Who this will benefit: Any business owner or professional who wants EXCELLENT LEADS and LOWER OVERALL MARKETING COSTS will benefit from this program.

Applications:

◆ Excellent for **locating and connecting with good prospects** from lead sources unknown to your competitors, which makes you a *"category of one."*

◆ Excellent for **developing inbound interest** from highly qualified prospects who are ideal to benefit from your premium products or services.

◆ Excellent for weeding out tire-kickers and **identifying excellent prospects**.

Problem this solves: This program separates suspects from prospects. It identifies people who self-select as prospects by responding to a direct mail letter and ask for more information. It helps ensure your more comprehensive direct response campaigns sent by FedEx and direct mail will be more cost-effective with a predictably higher ROI.

The Smart Start Program offers an opportunity for those professional executives who want to attract prospects who know **who you are** and **what you do**. This program eliminates those looky-loos AND identifies prospects who fit your avatar.

eLaunchers'
Direct-Connect
HANDWRITTEN

· · · · · · ·

Connect – Engage – Build Awareness – Sell

THE DIRECT-CONNECT HANDWRITTEN marketing platform is a monthly communications bundle consisting of handwritten letters, cards, newsletters, postcards, and marketing communications of nearly every variety.

It's a great way to personalize your communications **IN YOUR HANDWRITING**. It's an annualized bundle of more than 30 direct mail pieces specifically designed for high response levels. It can be used for client retention or lead generation.

Snapshot: Direct-Connect HANDWRITTEN is a 100% DONE-FOR-YOU bank of more than 30 machine-written marketing assets *that are virtually indistinguishable from HANDWRITTEN copy*. These assets, which mail monthly, include professionally written short sales letters, monthly greeting cards, a birthday and anniversary card, 12 short newsletters, and more.

Purpose: With more than 30 handwritten touchpoints delivered by U.S. Mail throughout the year, the purpose of Direct-Connect HANDWRITTEN is to (1) keep your name in front of your prospects and (2) build and maintain **TOP-OF-THE-MIND AWARE-NESS** with prospects.

Ideal for: Direct-Connect is ideal for any business or professional who wants to establish and maintain a strong awareness with their prospects by staying in touch throughout the year. ***So when it's time to buy, they think of you.***

What Direct-Connect accomplishes for you: With more than 30 personalized touchpoints going out automatically throughout the year, your prospects will feel like they KNOW, LIKE, and TRUST you.

Who will benefit: Any business owner or professional with a prospect list and a desire to keep in touch with those prospects will benefit from Direct-Connect. So when the time comes to buy, they will buy from you.

Direct-Connect is a PERFECT TOOL to (1) stay in touch, (2) build TOP-OF-THE-MIND AWARENESS with prospects, and (3) get MAXIMUM VALUE from your prospect list.

Applications:

◆ Maintain regular, personalized **contact** with your database of prospects.
◆ Build a strong sense of awareness with your prospects that

will, with many, eventually result in a sale that may never happen otherwise.

♦ **Breathe new life** into unconverted leads from your database (which may result in them contacting you) instead of those leads just sitting idle in your database gathering dust.

Use for all-source new lead follow-up *(trade shows, Web, radio, print, etc.).*

Problem this solves: People buy WHEN THEY ARE READY TO BUY—not when you are ready to sell. That is a fundamental sales principle.

One way or another, you pay for every lead in your database.

Only a small percentage of your prospects are ready to buy the first time you encounter them. And that makes following up with them one of the most important and potentially most valuable things you can do to increase your sales and build your business.

Direct-Connect HANDWRITTEN is a powerful, systematic, **SET-IT-AND-FORGET-IT** way to deliver a series of personalized, handwritten, professionally created messages to your prospects throughout the year. That's so when it's time to buy, **THEY THINK OF YOU.** "There are ways to use robotics to have handwritten messages written on paper with a real pen without using human labor.

If you do not have an effective, systematic way to stay in touch with your prospects throughout the year, Direct-Connect HAND-WRITTEN may be a perfect marketing asset for you.

There is much more I could share with you, but space is limited within the pages of this book.

To book a call with me, Parthiv Shah, to discuss systems, processes, discovering YOUR iceberg, building YOUR ship, or anything else, go to https://elaunchers.com/client and pick a day and time from my appointment calendar that works best for you. Or you can reach out to me by e-mail at pshah@elaunchers.com.

The Ultimate Gift from Parthiv and Rodger

. . . .

THANK YOU FOR reading this book. I hope you found it useful. Rodger and Parthiv are grateful for your continued interest.

We would like to continue this conversation with you. We encourage you to call our office at 301-760-3953 or visit <u>www.elaunchers.com/client</u> and book an appointment with Parthiv. At the designated time, you and Parthiv will talk about your practice and look at what Rodger and other financial advisors have done to propel their practices. We'll talk about what you can possibly do to adopt some of these principles in your practice.

At the end of your meeting, Parthiv will arrange to ship a box of books, a workbook, and other digital gifts on audio CDs, video DVDs, and a USB drive. These digital assets may be just the help you need to set your business on the path of success.

GET THE "ICEBERG" BINDER

Implement The Marketing System For
Financial Advisors In Your Practice Today!

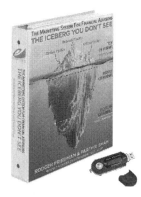

DEAR Financial Advisor,

Rodger and I have been putting together the "Iceberg" binder so we can share the best parts of our work in marketing for financial advisors.

We went through YEARS of archives in Rodger's library and my library and round up what has worked for Rodger and my other clients in past. We put all those assets in one organized binder and put all digital assets on a USB drive so someone who has resources to customize and implement everything can bring the "Iceberg" binder to life in their practice.

You will probably not implement everything. You might not implement ANYTHING. Learning what works can be very helpful. You may refer to this binder when you are in need of resources available nowhere else and you actually want to DO something.

I own elaunchers.com. We are a full service direct response marketing agency. We become your outsourced marketing department.

Depending on your situation, you might need a competent team of people who can move in and actually DO everything so you can focus on doing what you do best.

If that is you, congratulations! You are in the right place. We can be your marketing department and implementing the "Iceberg" binder will be what we will do together.

Either way, we should talk. Don't you want to look inside the binder and see what has worked for Rodger and my other clients?

To get started, please schedule a one hour online meeting with me at **www.elaunchers.com/client**.

13236 Executive Park Terrace
Germantown, MD 20874
www.elaunchers.com

pshah@elaunchers.com
Mobile: 301.873.5791
Direct: 301.760.3953

Made in the USA
Lexington, KY
10 December 2019